AROUND THE WORLD IN...

1800

AROUND THE WORLD IN...

1800

by Ruth Ashby

BENCHMARK BOOKS

MARSHALL CAVENDISH
NEW YORK

45575822

8/05

With thanks to J. Brett McClain of the Oriental Institute,
University of Chicago, for his careful reading of the manuscript

---

To my mom

• • •

Benchmark Books
Marshall Cavendish
99 White Plains Road
Tarrytown, New York 10591-9001
www.marshallcavendish.com

• • •

Library of Congress Cataloging-in-Publication Data
Ashby, Ruth.
1800/by Ruth Ashby.
p. cm—(Around the world in—)
Summary: Surveys important occurrences in Europe, Africa, Asia,
Australia and the Americas around the year 1800.
Includes bibliographical references and index.
ISBN 0-7614-1084-8 (lib. bdg.)
1. Eighteen hundred, A.D.—Juvenile literature.
2. Civilization, Modern—19th century—Juvenile literature.
[1. Eighteen hundred, A.D. 2. Nineteenth century. 3. World history.]
I. Title: Eighteen hundred. II. Title. III. Series.

CB417 .A84 2001   909.8—dc21   00-065136

• • •

Printed in Italy
1 3 5 6 4 2

• • •

Book Designer: Judith Turziano
Photo Research: Rose Corbett Gordon, Mystic CT

• • •

half title: A coal mine in England, around 1800.
title page: *Left*: Marie Antoinette surrounded by courtiers in a room of the
palace of Versailles, 1777; *Right*: Two French army volunteers.

• • •

CREDITS
Front cover: (left) Giraudon/Art Resource, NY; (right top) The Granger Collection, New York; (right bottom) Scala/Art Resource, NY
Back cover: (top) Private Collection/Bridgeman Art Library; (bottom) Japan Archive

Page 1: Walker Art Gallery, Liverpool, Trustees of the National Museums & Galleries on Merseyside;
page 2, 3, 13, 55: Giraudon/Art Resource, NY; page 6, 17: Louvre, Paris/Peter Willi/Bridgeman Art Library;
page 11, 14: Reunion des Musées Nationaux/Art Resource, NY; page 19: Tate Gallery, London/Art Resource, NY;
page 21: The Art Archive/Bibliothèque des Arts Décoratifs Paris/Dagli Orti (A); page 23: Guildhall Library,
Corporation of London/Bridgeman Art Library; page 25: Archivo Iconografico/Corbis; page 26 (top): Kaveler/Art Resource, NY;
page 26 (bottom) 42-43, 45, 78, 81, 89: The Granger Collection, New York; page 28, 29: Historisches Museum der Stadt, Vienna/Bridgeman
Art Library; page 33: The Art Archive/Musée des Arts Africains et Océaniens/Dagli Orti; page 34: Scala/Art Resource, NY;
page 35: British Library/Bridgeman Art Library; page 36: The Art Archive; page 38: Michael Graham-Stewart/Private Collection/Bridgeman
Art Library; page 39: York City Art Gallery/Bridgeman Art Library; page 46, 50: Stapleton Collection, UK/Bridgeman Art Library;
page 48-49: The Art Archive/ Eileen Tweedy; page 57: The Art Archive/Victoria and Albert Museum London/Sally Chappell;
page 59: The Art Archive/Turkish and Islamic Art Museum Istanbul/Dagli Orti (A); page 61: Japan Archives; page 62: Pushkin Museum,
Moscow/Bridgeman Art Library; page 63: Historical Picture Archive/Corbis; page 64: School of Oriental & African Studies Library,
University of London/Bridgeman Art Library; page 69, 71, 73: Private Collection/Bridgeman Art Library; page 70: Werner Forman/Art
Resource, NY; page 77: New-York Historical Society/Bridgeman Art Library; page 82, 86: Bettmann/Corbis; page 83: North Wind Picture Archives;
page 85: J.P. Zenobel/Galerie Mona Lisa, Paris/Bridgeman Art Library; page 87: Military Museum, Caracas/Photo by Christopher Ralling

CONTENTS

Napoleon crossing the Alps on 20 May, 1800. This splendidly romantic painting by Napoleon's favorite artist, Jacques-Louis David, captures the energy and power of the young conqueror.

INTRODUCTION

The time is 1800. In Europe, a brilliant French general is leading his troops over the Alps to conquer a neighboring nation—and then, he hopes, the world. On the southern tip of Africa, a boy is tending cattle and dreaming of becoming a warrior. In Australia, a group of convicts are starting a new life on a strange, distant shore. In North America, an ex-slave is leading a revolution. From continent to continent, things are happening.

If you could board a time machine and get off at 1800, these are some of the things you would witness. Most people learn about history by focusing on just one country or place. Most of the time, they learn about events only from their own perspective, that is, from the point of view of their nation or heritage. This is certainly a valid way to try to understand the world, but it can be narrow and one-sided. In this book, we thought it might be worthwhile to take a different approach to history, by looking at events that were occurring all across the world at one period of time. Around 1800, the world was connected as never before—by war, by trade, and by the exchange of ideas. Perhaps if we take this broader, "bird's-eye" view of history, we can understand how what happened two hundred years ago helped make us the way we are today.

So step aboard our "time machine" and get ready to take a trip around the world.

EUROPE AROUND 1800

Atlantic
Ocean

GREAT
BRITAIN

London

HOLLAND

PRUSSIA

RUSSIA

Battle of
Waterloo

Paris

FRANCE

AUSTRIA

Vienna

A L P s

PORTUGAL

SPAIN

CORSICA

Mediterranean Sea

N
W   E
S

Miles   0   200   500

Kilometers 0   400   800

PART I
EUROPE

Two hundred years ago, Europe was changing—fast. In politics, the French Revolution of 1789 had toppled a king and overthrown a ruling class. In technology, the Industrial Revolution was building amazing machinery and transforming lives. In the arts, the Romantic revolution was creating art, music, and literature for a new age.

Europe thought it was the most important place in the world—and in a sense, it was. In 1800, no other continent had such widespread influence. From Venezuela to India to Australia, European power, European ideas, and European trade dislocated people, inspired revolutions, and changed traditional ways of life. Napoleon Bonaparte, the dictator who grabbed power in France after the Revolution was over, started a war in Europe that spread to distant continents. The Napoleonic Wars have been called the first world war. Distant places and peoples came together in new and unexpected ways. This was an age in which a man like General Charles Cornwallis could be born in Britain, fight in America, serve in Prussia, and die in India.

The pace of change sped up in the nineteenth century—and it has never slowed down.

IMPORTANT DATES

France—The Revolutionary Era
1789–1815

England—The Industrial Revolution
c. 1730–1850

Germany—The Romantic Age
c. 1770-1848

FRANCE
REVOLUTION!

If there had been a *Time* magazine in 1800, Napoleon Bonaparte (1769–1821) would have been Man of the Year. In February, he became first consul of the French republic. In May, he crossed the Alps with his army and defeated Austria in a brilliant battle.

But he was just getting started. Four years later, Napoleon was proclaimed emperor. Now he ruled France. But he wanted to rule the world.

It was a miracle he had come so far. Napoleon Bonaparte was born on August 15, 1769, on Corsica, an island in the Mediterranean. His family was of the minor nobility, with little social standing and less money. Young Napoleon was a sickly child with a bad temper. When he didn't get his way, he would scream, kick, scratch, and hit. "I was always spoiling for a fight," he remembered later.

Napoleon always knew he wanted to become a soldier. When he was nine, he was sent to military school in France. His schoolmates taunted the shabby boy and called him the "Corsican savage." Napoleon fought back with his fists. Today we would say he had a behavior problem. Although he made few friends, he did well at school, especially in math and science. At the end of his training, he was named a second lieutenant in an artillery (cannon) regiment.

In ordinary times, Napoleon's career would have been mapped out for him. Because his family wasn't rich or important, he would have risen slowly through the ranks. After thirty years, he might have retired as a captain.

But these were not ordinary times. In 1789, France was engulfed in revolution. And nothing would ever be the same again.

France before the Revolution (called the ancien régime, or "old order")

The storming of the Bastille, July 14, 1789. Although by 1789 the old fortress was seldom used, it remained a hated symbol of royal oppression. After the revolutionaries seized the fortress and opened the dungeon, they found only seven people still imprisoned.

was a land of extremes: great poverty and great wealth, fabulous luxury and desperate hardship. The population was divided into three social classes, called estates. The First Estate was the clergy; the Second Estate was the nobility. Although together they made up only 4 percent of the population, these two groups had all of the power and most of the wealth of the kingdom.

Everyone else was a member of the Third Estate. The 24 million peasants were desperately poor. Families of nine or ten lived in one-room huts and starved. There was never enough to eat. A series of bad harvests in the 1780s led to a shortage of bread, the basic food. Eventually the price of bread was so high it used up half a worker's wages.

At the top of the social pyramid was the king of France, Louis XVI, and his wife, Marie Antoinette. The king was fat, lazy, and not very bright. The queen had a reputation for extravagance—she owned one thousand dresses—and selfishness. (When told the peasants were starving because there was no bread, she was said to have remarked, "Let them eat cake." Although modern historians doubt the queen ever said this, rumors of these kinds of callous remarks made her hated throughout the kingdom.)

By the late 1780s, the government was almost bankrupt. Bread riots broke out around the countryside. The government needed to raise taxes, but the First and Second Estates refused to pay their share.

France was on the verge of chaos. What could be done?

Under pressure, King Louis XVI called a meeting of all three estates to decide how to save the country. Reformers wanted power to be shared more equally among all the people. But soon it became clear that the king would not accept real changes in the way France was governed. The representatives of the Third Estate decided to break away from the convention and form their own separate National Assembly. They started to write a new constitution for the country.

Then, on July 14, 1789, the people took matters into their own hands. Crowds stormed the Bastille, an ancient royal prison in Paris. The French Revolution had begun.

Soon the slogan of the Revolution—*Liberté, Égalité, Fraternité* (Liberty, Equality, Fraternity)—was on everyone's lips. Across Europe, people celebrated the beginning of a new era. To idealistic young people especially, the Revolution was a wonderful event. "Bliss was it in that dawn to be alive," the poet William Wordsworth wrote. "But to be young was very heaven."

A few months later, the assembly was ready with a new constitution. The Declaration of the Rights of Man and Citizen declared that "men are born and remain free and equal in rights" and that the "source of all sovereignty resides in the people." Despite the wording of the declaration,

French revolutionaries were called sansculottes, which meant they were "without breeches," the short knee-pants worn by members of the nobility. To liberal democrats in the United States and Europe, the sansculottes were freedom fighters; to conservatives, they were dangerous fanatics.

it still looked as though the king would be able to keep his throne and share power with the other branches of government.

But that was not to be. Unwilling to give up his power, Louis XVI asked for the help of other European monarchs to fight the revolutionaries. As Prussian and Austrian armies crossed the French border, popular unrest grew. Extremists saw enemies everywhere and encouraged the common people to riot. Mobs massacred thousands of presumed royalist sympathizers.

Soon the radicals took over the Revolution. In 1793 the king and queen were beheaded. A new queen of terror reigned: La Guillotine, an efficient machine of death that sliced off the heads of anyone suspected of not supporting the Revolution. More than ten thousand people died during the period that came

Napoleon watches his cavalry charge into combat at the Battle of Wagram, July 6, 1809. The engagement completed his conquest of Austria. By 1811, Napoleon controlled most of Europe, from Spain in the west to the Grand Duchy of Warsaw (Poland) in the east.

to be called the Reign of Terror, 1793–1794.

European royalty was alarmed. This bloodthirsty revolutionary spirit could be catching. Austria, Prussia, Spain, England, and Holland united in an alliance against France. The revolutionaries found themselves fighting revolts within the country and invasions from without.

Enter Napoleon. In 1789, he was a second lieutenant in an artillery regiment in the south of France. Like other young men of the age, Napoleon at first supported the ideals of the Revolution. But after he saw a mob massacre a group of royal guards, he became disillusioned. Without the right kind of leadership, he thought, the people were uncontrolled savages. They must be led.

It was the perfect opportunity for an ambitious young man to build his career. Soon a series of brilliant victories against the invading European armies had catapulted Napoleon from lieutenant to captain to general. His victories made him famous all over France. When the French government seemed on the verge of collapse ten years after the Revolution began, Napoleon made himself dictator and announced, "Citizens...the Revolution is ended."

It hadn't actually ended. The ideals of the Revolution—Liberty, Equality, Fraternity—continued to inspire people around the world for the next century. But the fighting had stopped.

And what of Napoleon? During the next few years, he established his own personal brand of revolution. To a nation tired of fighting, he brought peace. To a people weary of chaos, he brought order. In a very short period of time, he rehabilitated France and brought it into the nineteenth century. He built factories, canals, harbors, bridges, tunnels, and roads. He began to modernize Paris and turn it into a cultural capital. His wars created new jobs and started new industries.

His most important legacy was a new system of laws, called the Napoleonic Code. It took the ideas of the Revolution—liberty and equality—and made them law. All men (but not women) were equal before the law. All could own property and choose their own occupation or religion. The code was so influential that it later became the basis of many legal systems around the world.

But Napoleon could never rest on his achievements. He was driven to keep fighting—and winning. Between 1805 and 1815, while he tried to become emperor of the world, he led his troops into battle against every major European power. He slashed through Spain, Portugal, Prussia, Austria, Italy, and Russia, spreading death and devastation. "Boney," as the British called him, was universally feared and hated. "You better

NEW CLOTHES FOR A NEW AGE

In the early days of the French Revolution, clothes could be dangerous. People were killed just for the way they dressed. Powdered wigs, tight breeches (knee-pants), brocades and velvet all marked the wearer as aristocratic and therefore dangerous. Revolutionaries—called sansculottes, or "without breeches"—wore baggy striped pants, white shirts, and red caps. Women wore striped skirts and plain bonnets. Everyone wore red rosettes in their hats—or risked being labeled antirevolutionary.

Napoleon Bonaparte, while still a minor officer, tried escorting his sister Elisa from boarding school in France back to their home in Corsica. Crowds stormed their carriage when they saw Elisa's fashionable clothes. Napoleon had to show them the red rosette in his hat—and shout some revolutionary slogans—before the crowds let them pass.

The most radical days of the Revolution were over by 1794. But the revolution in fashion continued. It was trendy to wear clothes modeled on those of the ancient Greeks, who founded the first democracy. These clothes were freer, lighter, and more comfortable than earlier styles. Gone were the confining corsets, belts, bustles, and petticoats of the eighteenth century. Women wore sheer dresses that fell freely to the feet. The waistline came just below the bust, and the neckline fell just above it. For a few years, dresses were so flimsy and transparent they were practically see-through. Gone, too, were the heavy powdered wigs

behave yourself," mothers would warn their children, "or Boney will come and get you!"

By the time Napoleon was defeated for the last time, at the Battle of Waterloo in 1815, everyone longed for peace. Boney was exiled to the rocky island of Saint Helena, where he died a few years later. And the European heads of state met at the Congress of Vienna in 1814–1815 to restore Europe

In Jacques-Louis David's **Madame Raymond de Verninac** *(1799), the sitter wears a simple Greek-inspired frock with a high waist and has dressed her hair in natural-looking ringlets.*

of Louis XVI and Marie Antoinette. Women wore their hair in the Grecian style, with a fringe on the forehead and ringlets about the face.

Luxury made a comeback with Napoleon's court. But even though silks and velvets replaced cottons and muslins, comfortable styles remained.

Women's clothes would not be so free and comfortable again until the 1920s. As the nineteenth century progressed, corsets and petticoats came back into style. It would take another revolution in dress to bring us the blue jeans of the twentieth century.

Vive la revolution!

to its pre-French Revolution condition. Even Louis XVIII, brother of the beheaded king, was brought back to sit on the French throne. The old order was reestablished. Everyone breathed a sigh of relief.

Not for long. During the next hundred years, monarchies toppled, new nations were formed, and age-old ways of life came to an end. The spirit of the French Revolution lived on.

ENGLAND
IRON, COAL, AND STEAM

In 1800, another important revolution was occurring—probably the most important ever. No, it was not the American Revolution. It was the Industrial Revolution, and it transformed the world.

Imagine living on a small farmstead in Europe sometime around 1730. Your cottage has dirt floors and wattle-and-daub walls. There is no running water, no electricity, no stove, and no toilet. One-quarter of your children die before their first birthday, and you yourself have a life expectancy of only about forty years. You are dependent on nature for survival. If the crops fail, you go hungry. The only power available to you other than your own muscles is that of your animals, and of wind and water.

It was a kind of life that philosopher Thomas Hobbes called "nasty, brutish, and short," and it was the way eight out of ten Europeans lived in 1730. It was the way they had lived for thousands of years.

Suddenly there was the Industrial Revolution. Goods were made by power-driven machinery instead of by hand; many people worked in factories instead of at home. Amazing innovations changed people's lives forever—railroads, steamships, the telegraph, photography, electricity.

It all started in Britain in the eighteenth century.

Why Britain? There were lots of reasons. Britain had large deposits of coal available for industrial fuel and a large workforce to mine it. It had a thriving trading business and lots of overseas markets in which to buy and sell goods. And it was isolated from mainland Europe, so it was protected from Continental wars.

Just as important, Britain had a large middle-class population. Because they are educated but not wealthy, members of the middle class have to

As his family looks on, a blacksmith and his assistant work a white-hot piece of metal in An Iron Forge (1772), by Joseph Wright of Derby. By the late 1700s, Britain had a thriving iron industry: mines where iron ore was dug, foundries where ore was smelted into metal, and forges where iron was hammered into tools and horseshoes.

work for a living, unlike the aristocracy. Most modern inventors (and scientists, writers, artists, and musicians) have been middle class.

And why did the Industrial Revolution begin in the eighteenth century? For one thing, there were more people. The death rate fell as ancient

THE IRON HORSE

The Industrial Revolution would not have happened without the railroad. Railroads moved goods and people cheaply across countries and continents. No one born in 1850 could have imagined life without them.

Railroads actually existed before the steam locomotive. In coal mines in Europe and Britain, horses pulled carts of coal along wooden tracks centuries before James Watt developed a workable steam engine. (No wonder the early locomotive was called an "iron horse.") In 1804, Richard Trevithick adapted Watt's engine to locomotives and developed the first steam-powered railway engine. A few years later, he demonstrated his engine in London. For a shilling, people could ride the locomotive *Catch-Me-Who-Can* around a circular track—at twelve miles per hour!

Unfortunately, Trevithick's engines had a tendency to break down. The first really reliable locomotive was built by another Englishman, George Stephenson. In 1829, his *Rocket* won an engine competition sponsored by the Liverpool and Manchester Railway, which was just being built. Before an enthusiastic crowd of 15,000, the *Rocket* reached speeds of thirty-two miles per hour. A year later, the Liverpool and Manchester Railway officially opened—and the railroad age began.

plagues such as the Black Death disappeared. A smallpox vaccine was developed in the 1770s. Food was more plentiful, due to the introduction of new crops such as potatoes and corn. Sheep were bred to be fatter and healthier. New seed drills planted more seed.

More people demanded more goods—goods that could be made faster and more economically. Take cloth, for instance. Cloth had been one of England's main products for centuries. But the path from sheep to finished coat was very long. First the sheep would be sheared and the wool would be cleaned by hand. Then it was transported by horse to a cottage, where

English actress Fanny Kemble has left us an account of what it was like to ride the rails in 1830:

> The engine set off at its utmost speed, 35 miles an hour, swifter than a bird flies…. You cannot conceive what the sensation of cutting the air was…. I stood up with my bonnet off "and drank the air before me."… When I closed my eyes this sensation of flying was quite delightful, and strange beyond description.

By 1855, there were almost 12,000 miles of track in Great Britain.

George Stephenson's **Rocket** *adapted James Watt's double-action steam engine and demonstrated that locomotives were fast and dependable.*

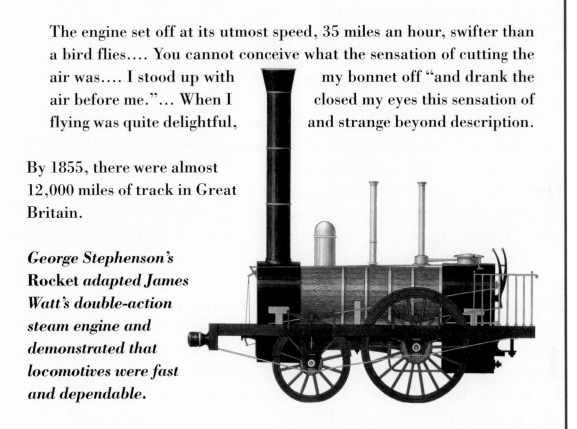

women and children would spin it by hand into thread. The thread would be sent to a weaver, who would weave it on a loom by hand, and the cloth would go to a tailor, who then cut and sewed it by hand. No wonder only the wealthy could afford more than one coat or dress every few years.

English inventors changed all that. In 1733, John Kay invented the flying shuttle, a machine that allowed the weaver to work twice as fast. In 1764, James Hargreaves developed the spinning jenny, which allowed a spinner to make ten, twenty, or one hundred threads at once. And in 1779, Samuel Crompton made a machine called a mule, which allowed the spinning jenny to work even faster.

These machines were still made of wood, not metal, and they relied on muscle power or waterpower. But scientists and inventors were fascinated by the possibilities. Who would take the machine a step further? And how would he do it?

The answer came from a quiet Scottish instrument maker who worked for decades to develop a usable steam engine. James Watt (1736–1819) had been a sickly child. During his long hours in bed, he amused himself by fixing broken toys for all the children in the neighborhood. Eventually his genius at working with his hands led him to a lifetime of invention.

Watt's steam engine operated by condensing water. He received a patent for his machine in 1769, but it was many years before he had enough money to actually build and sell it. First he needed partners to invest in his ideas.

Investors were plentiful in England in the last decades of the eighteenth century. Overseas trade—in tea, cloth, gold, rum, and slaves—had made many businessmen very wealthy. They looked for ways to make even more money. Today they might buy shares on the stock exchange. Two hundred years ago, they invested their money in land or livestock, or, more often, in industry.

Eventually Watt teamed up with a rich industrialist to manufacture his invention. By 1800, their company had sold five hundred steam engines. The engines powered Crompton's mules and power looms. They ran machines in paper and flour mills. They also ran pumps to draw water out of coal mines so that workers could dig deeper than ever, below the water table. As more industrial uses were found for the steam engine, England produced more goods and more wealth.

The Industrial Revolution came to the United States soon thereafter, and then to western Europe after the Napoleonic Wars. But the British had gotten a huge head start. In 1851, they put on a show to boast about their accomplishments. Queen Victoria proudly opened the Great Exhibition of the Works of Industry of All Nations at the Crystal Palace in London. The United States had 500 displays (among them, false teeth,

The spectacularly successful Crystal Palace exhibition in London drew 6,200,000 visitors in six months. Among the manufactured products exhibited for the first time were steam engines, the McCormick reaper, weapons, matches, envelopes, and the yellow pencil.

artificial legs, the McCormick reaper, and Goodyear india rubber). But Britain had more than 12,000 exhibits—big machines including hydraulic presses, pumps, and automated cotton-spinning mules.

In the first half of the nineteenth century, Britain was the workshop of the world.

GERMANY
THE ART OF ROMANTICISM

In 1812, two of the greatest geniuses of the age, Johann Wolfgang von Goethe (1749–1832) and Ludwig van Beethoven (1770–1827), were taking a stroll in the public gardens of Teplitz, Austria. They saw the empress of Austria approaching with members of her court. "Now keep your arm linked in mine," Beethoven instructed the older man. "They must make way for us, not we for them." Goethe couldn't help himself. He automatically stepped aside to let the nobility pass. Beethoven, though, crossed his arms and plowed right through the crowd. He was an Artist, after all—and he was quite sure that artists were superior to mere dukes.

Beethoven was a leading figure in yet another revolution sweeping through Europe in the early 1800s—the Romantic revolution. Like other cultural movements, this one didn't involve armies or dictators, although it was influenced by the huge political upheavals of the time. Romanticism was all about the power of the imagination. It put the highest value on revelations of the human spirit—whether in art, music, or poetry. Romantic artists created works of deep emotional intensity and, they thought, supreme importance. "Poets are the unacknowledged legislators [leaders] of the world," poet Percy Bysshe Shelley proclaimed.

Romanticism first sprang up on the Continent, especially in Germany. In the early 1800s, Germany wasn't a real nation. It was actually a hodge-podge of duchies, principalities, and cities, dominated by two large states, Prussia and Austria, and bound by a common language and culture. Each state was ruled by a hereditary ruler. Naturally, these rulers were terrified by the French Revolution—and despised Napoleon as a lower-class usurper. Any kind of political dissension was immediately suppressed

This famous portrait of Ludwig van Beethoven painted by Joseph Carl Stieler in 1820 shows the inspired artist writing one of his last works, a choral piece entitled Missa Solemnis.

Goethe in the Campagna *(1787) by J.H.W. Tischbein, places the author in an imaginary landscape of Roman ruins. The painting suggests that Goethe's writing is based on classical models and will someday achieve the immortality of Greek and Roman art.*

The title page of Goethe's novel **The Sorrows of Young Werther** *portrays the hero in a love-sick reverie.* **Werther** *was probably the first international best-seller. By 1800, it was read everywhere, from the salons of St. Petersburg to the drawing rooms of Boston.*

in Germany. Real change came not in politics, but in the arts.

The first glimmers of Romanticism could be seen in the late eighteenth century, when Goethe wrote *The Sorrows of Young Werther*. In 1774, this emotional novel became a runaway best-seller. It tells the melancholy tale of a young man who falls in love with a married woman, is rejected, and commits suicide. Werther became the first teenage role model. Suddenly, like Werther, young men from Russia to England were wearing blue tailcoats and yellow vests and fainting at the sight of their beloved. Luckily, few of them committed suicide.

The book launched Goethe on the road to fame and success. Eventually his masterpieces led people to class him with Homer, Shakespeare, Cervantes, and other literary greats.

But Goethe, who was of the pre-Revolutionary generation, still felt he had to defer to royalty. Beethoven, who came of age during the French Revolution, believed that all men were equal—except for geniuses (such as himself), who were superior.

Beethoven was a tormented genius. His main problem was that he was going deaf, and as he got older, he couldn't even hear his own music. Today we know that he had a disease in which the cartilage of the inner ear turns slowly into bone. He was tortured by whistling and ringing in his ears. By the time he was forty-seven, he was stone-deaf—and truly eccentric. Untidy and quarrelsome, with greasy hair and a pockmarked face, he would walk the streets of Vienna, humming to himself and waving his arms wildly.

Yet everyone agreed that he wrote the most sublime music they had ever heard. Beethoven believed that he was divinely inspired: "I know well that God is nearer to me in my art than to others."

"Music," he once claimed, "is a greater revelation than the whole of wisdom and philosophy." Beethoven's music was more dramatic than anything anyone had heard before. It soared in ecstasy and plunged in despair. Into it Beethoven poured all the joy, rage, hope, and longing of his soul.

Like Mozart and Haydn before him, Beethoven lived in Vienna, the

Vienna as Beethoven might have seen it from his window in 1825. This walled city contained ballrooms, opera houses, orchestras, choirs, and many of the best musicians in the world.

music capital of Europe. He was there in 1815 when, after Napoleon finally had been defeated, representatives of all the major European powers came to town. Russians, English, Austrians, Italians, Prussians, and French were there to reorganize Europe—and to have a good time. Beethoven gave five major concerts for the star-studded gathering. He was the first international music celebrity—a short, stout, deaf man whose music moved the heavens.

When Beethoven died in 1827, 20,000 people came to his funeral. He wrote his own epitaph: "What more can be given to man than fame and praise and immortality?"

DO I HEAR A WALTZ?

Picture a grand ballroom. Lights are blazing, the orchestra is playing, the dancers are spinning around and around. One, two, three…one, two, three…

They are dancing the waltz, the most romantic dance of all time. Originally a folk dance from Austria and Germany, the waltz made its first appearance in the courts of Europe around 1800. It caused an immediate sensation. Traditional ballroom dances such as the minuet and gavotte were formal and intricate. Male and female partners performed the complex figures at arm's length, coming together only to separate again at the next beat.

But in the waltz, a man actually had his arms around the woman—*for the whole dance!* Polite society was outraged. When the waltz was introduced in England in 1816, a writer for the *Times* fumed, "We remarked with pain that the indecent foreign dance called the Waltz was introduced (we believe for the first time) at the English court on Friday last…. We feel it a duty to warn every parent against exposing his daughter to so fatal a contagion."

But the waltz was immediately and overwhelmingly popular. There were nearly seven hundred dance halls in Paris alone after the Revolution. In 1804, a German visitor remarked, "This love for the waltz and this adoption of the German dance is quite new and has become one of the vulgar fashions since the war, like smoking."

Vienna during the congress in 1814–1815 was simply waltz-mad. Diplomats who planned the future of Europe in the morning spent their evenings waltzing around a ballroom at dizzying speed: One, two, three…one, two, three…

Following its introduction in Vienna, the waltz became the most popular dance in Europe.

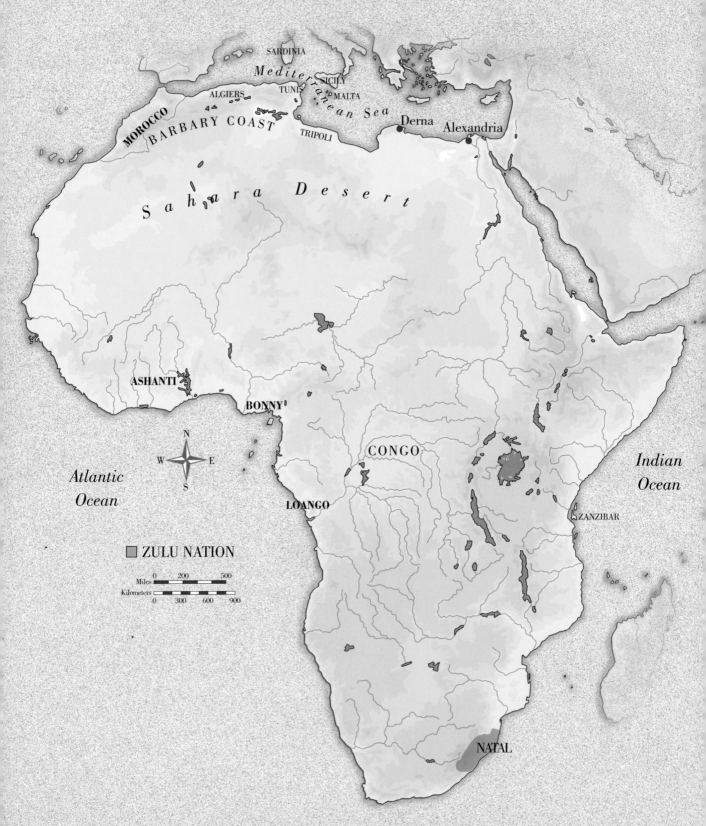

AFRICA AROUND 1800

SARDINIA

Mediterranean Sea

SICILY

TUNIS

MALTA

ALGIERS

MOROCCO

BARBARY COAST

TRIPOLI

Derna

Alexandria

S a h a r a   D e s e r t

ASHANTI

BONNY

CONGO

N
W · E
S

*Atlantic
Ocean*

*Indian
Ocean*

LOANGO

ZANZIBAR

☐ ZULU NATION

Miles
0   200   500

Kilometers
0   300   600   900

NATAL

PART II

AFRICA

The huge continent of Africa has always been divided by the immense Sahara Desert, thick jungles, and broad plains. But in 1800, it was united as never before—by the slave trade. From the coastline of Ghana to the jungles of the Congo to the island of Zanzibar, people were captured, sold, and transported. The African slave trade was not new—it had always existed within Africa, around the Mediterranean, and in the Middle East. But with the coming of European traders, it was accelerated, and now it affected the rest of the world.

Within the African interior, many people were still in communities cut off from the wider world. There, lives were lived and wars were fought with little interference from the outside. European exploration and trade changed all that as the nineteenth century progressed. But for now, African kings ruled supreme in their own lands.

IMPORTANT DATES

West Africa—The Slave Trade
1492–1870

North Africa—The Barbary War
1801–1805

South Africa—The Zulu Kingdom
1816–1880

WEST AFRICA
SLAVE TRADERS AND SLAVES

To the rest of the world, Africa in 1800 meant one thing: slaves. Yes, the continent offered other goods, too—ivory, gold, spices, cloth. But the main commodity was human beings. Between 1492 and 1870, about 11 million human beings were shipped from West Africa across the Atlantic Ocean to the Americas. Over a still longer period of time, another 9 million people were taken from East Africa to Islamic lands to the north and east.

The extent of the African slave trade was extraordinary, but slavery was not new. It had always existed in human history. There were slaves in ancient Greece and Rome, slaves in Egypt, slaves in China and Mexico before Columbus. There had always been slavery throughout Africa and the Middle East. But by the 1400s, slavery had pretty much disappeared from northern Europe and was relatively unimportant in southern Europe.

That all changed when Europeans began to colonize the New World in the early sixteenth century. The tobacco, sugar, and cotton plantations they established needed lots of cheap labor. Native Americans, unused to farm work, died off quickly. So Europeans began to import the labor they needed from Africa.

Africans had a lot to recommend them. They were used to the hard work of planting, cultivating, and harvesting, since they came from mainly agricultural economies. And since Africa had always had a thriving slave trade, Europeans were able to find willing partners. African traders supplied the slaves, for Europeans seldom ventured into the interior. The African coast was known as the "white man's grave." Tropical diseases quickly killed off people without natural immunities.

The slave trade stripped the land of people. Men, women, and children

Slaves brought from the interior of Africa were forced to march in long trains called coffles and were often tied together by ropes, chains, or wooden yokes. They were traded for goods such as the gun held by the African slave trader on the right.

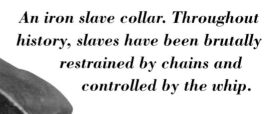

An iron slave collar. Throughout history, slaves have been brutally restrained by chains and controlled by the whip.

were kidnapped by gangs of African traders, captured in war, or punished for real or imagined crimes, and carried off forever. They made the trek from the interior to the coast in long caravans, or coffles, bound together by leather thongs or yokes. When they reached the shore, the traders would sell them to African middlemen—chiefs or wealthy businessmen—who would turn them over to the Europeans. Slaves were exchanged for European guns, liquor, tobacco, cloth, and other goods.

The captives' grief and terror can hardly be imagined. We have only a few firsthand accounts of what it was like to be kidnapped and sold as a slave. The best known is by a Nigerian named Olaudah Equiano, who published an account of his life in 1789.

"One day [at the age of eleven]," he recalled, "when all our people were gone out to their works, and only I and my dear sister were left to mind the house, two men and a woman got over our walls and in a moment seized us both.… The next day, my sister and I…were separated while we lay clasped in each other's arms."

Equiano never saw his sister again. He was sold from one trader to another and eventually ended up on the coast. There he saw "a slave ship…riding at anchor waiting for its cargo…. When I looked round the ship, and saw a large furnace, or copper boiling, and a multitude of black people of every description chained together, every one of their countenances expressing dejection and sorrow…, I asked if we were not to be eaten by those white men with horrible looks, red faces and long hair."

No, the strange white men were not cannibals. But for Equiano and the millions of other Africans en route

Olaudah Equiano,
or
GUSTAVUS VASSA,
the African.

Published March 1 1789 by G. Vassa

The frontispiece of The Life of Olaudah Equiano. *Equiano's true story of being kidnapped and sold as a slave opened many eyes to the horrors of the Atlantic slave trade. Unlike millions of his fellow sufferers, he was eventually freed and educated. Later, he returned to Africa as a missionary and abolitionist.*

Slaves were crammed into the ship's hold during the journey from Africa to the Americas, called the Middle Passage. Equiano remembered that on his voyage "each had scarcely room to turn himself, [and the heat] almost suffocated us."

to the Americas, the horrors had just begun.

European countries became wealthy on the slave trade. The port of Liverpool, England, it was said, was "built up by the blood of poor Africans." In 1800, about 120 Liverpool ships a year brought 35,000 slaves to the Americas. The trade gave business to the boatbuilders, coopers, grocers, carpenters, sail makers, and even to attorneys and tailors. The trade made many people prosperous, and some people rich.

All that extra money fueled the Industrial Revolution.

The African slave trade did not, however, make Africa rich. The profits of the trade went into the hands of the very few—kings and powerful merchants, especially in Angola, Ashanti, Benin, Loango, and the Congo. Most Africans remained subsistence herders and farmers. And although tribes had always fought among themselves, now more kings sought war in order to increase the number of captives they could sell. The firearms they bought from the Europeans made these kings more deadly, so that they were able to capture more slaves—and buy more guns. It was a vicious circle, and millions of ordinary Africans suffered horribly. The trade brutalized everyone—the Europeans who bought the slaves, the Africans who sold them, and everyone who was sold.

The transatlantic slave trade reached its peak in the decade before 1800—when nearly 500,000 slaves were transported. Then there was a gradual slowdown. After Britain went to war with France during the Revolution, French ships were prevented from trading. Then Britain, in 1807, and the United States, in 1808, abolished the slave trade (but not slavery). By then, the trade had already helped make Britain the richest nation on earth.

The kings of West Africa didn't want the trade to end. It was their main source of wealth. The king of Bonny told a Liverpool captain, "We think that this trade must go on. That is the verdict of our oracle and the priests. They say that your country, however great, can never stop a trade ordained by God himself." He didn't have to worry. The trade to Brazil went on until 1850, the trade to Cuba until 1870, and the East African slave trade until the twentieth century.

NORTH AFRICA
THE BARBARY PIRATES

For eight hundred years, the four states of the North African coast—Tripoli, Tunis, Algiers, and Morocco (modern-day Libya, Tunisia, Algeria, and Morocco)— had been making their living terrorizing ships in the Mediterranean Sea. Europeans called them barbarians, and the area became known as the Barbary Coast. Pirate ships launched from North African harbors attacked merchant ships, looting the cargo and capturing crews and passengers alike. Usually Christian ships were taken, for the Muslim pirates justified the piracy as a kind of religious war. Over the centuries, these corsairs, as the pirates and their ships were known, also raided the Mediterranean coast, kidnapping people from Italy, Malta, Sicily, Sardinia, and Corsica. In about 1700, there may have been 25,000 white Christian slaves in Algiers alone.

By the late eighteenth century, kidnapping and slavery were among

The "celebrated" pirate ship L'Antonio. Pirate ships were quick and light, designed to chase heavier merchant and naval vessels and capture them.

*With its white buildings, blue harbor, and green hills,
nineteenth-century Algiers was picturesque from a distance.
Americans captured by Algerian corsairs saw a different city:
narrow, filthy streets, stone prisons, and chain gangs.*

the main trades of North Africa. Every major town had its slave market,
where men, women, and children were displayed and haggled over. Men
could end up on the work gangs of local rulers, building roads or bridges.
Women became servants or concubines in local harems. The wealthy were
usually ransomed; money was put up by their family or community for
their release. Others, not so fortunate, could be subjected to a lifetime
of imprisonment and humiliation, in a world where severe punishment
and torture were routine.

For centuries, Western nations launched unsuccessful attacks upon
the cities of the Barbary Coast. England bowed to reality in 1646 and
began paying tribute in order to free English captives and prevent English

ships from being taken. Other European countries followed suit.

To many, it looked as if the West had just given in. In 1799, when British liberals were lobbying for an end to the African slave trade, Admiral Horatio Nelson wrote, "My blood boils that I cannot chastise these pirates. They could not show themselves in the Mediterranean did not our country permit. Never let us talk about the cruelty of the African slave-trade while we permit such a horrid war."

This was the situation when Thomas Jefferson became president of the United States. As long as the American colonies had been British, Britain had paid to protect their ships against the pirates. After the Revolutionary War, the new American government was forced to continue the tradition. William Eaton, American consul in Tunis, recorded that he gave the bey, or local ruler, one musket set with diamonds, four pairs of gold-mounted pistols, a diamond ring, and many other luxuries. By 1800, the Barbary states had demanded two million dollars in tribute from the United States—and they wanted more. In the meantime, Yankee sailors were still being kidnapped.

Jefferson had had enough. "I know that nothing will stop the eternal increase of demands from these pirates but the pressure of an armed force," he wrote his friend James Madison. He refused to pay any more—and Tripoli declared war against the United States.

The United States had just a small navy. Jefferson ordered it to North Africa, and in 1801 the fleet sailed into the Mediterranean. All went well until November 1803, when the frigate *Philadelphia* ran aground outside Tripoli. Pirates swarmed upon the decks and the crew was captured. Now the pirates had control of a modern warship. Who knew what they would do with it?

The situation was very dangerous. The Americans knew they couldn't recapture the ship. But perhaps they could destroy it.

The commander of the young navy, Edward Preble, had a plan. He sent a daring lieutenant named Stephen Decatur on an undercover mission.

On February 16, 1804, Decatur sailed an old freighter named the *Intrepid*

CAPTURED!

On November 1, 1803, 307 sailors on the U.S. *Philadelphia* were taken prisoner by Barbary pirates off the coast of Tripoli. Five years later, crew member William Ray published a narrative of his captivity entitled *Horrors of Slavery or the American Tars in Tripoli*. In it he recalled his first view of the city after they were rowed ashore:

> At the beach stood a row of armed men on either side of us, who passed us along to the castle gate. It opened, and we ascended a winding, narrow, dismal passage, which led into a paved avenue, lined with terrific jannisaries [guards], armed with glittering sabers, muskets, pistols, and tomahawks. Several of them spit on us as we passed. We were hurried forward through various turnings and flights of stairs, until we found ourselves in the dreadful presence of his exalted majesty, the puissant [powerful] Bashaw of Tripoli. His throne, on which he was seated, was...covered with a cushion of the richest velvet, fringed with cloth of gold, bespangled with brilliants.... The Bashaw made a very splendid...appearance. His vesture [clothing] was a long robe of cerulean silk, embroidered with gold and glittering with tinsel. His broad belt was ornamented with diamonds, and held two gold-mounted pistols, and a saber with a golden hilt, chain, and scabbard. On his head he wore a large white turban, decorated with ribbons.

This was the last time Ray was in the presence of such luxury. For the next nineteen months, he and his fellow sailors did hard labor repairing the stone walls of the city. They were not released until William Eaton captured Derna—and the United States paid a small ransom.

into Tripoli harbor. It had been disguised to look like a North African vessel. Hidden belowdecks were sixty-eight American sailors. When the freighter neared the captured warship, someone aboard the *Philadelphia* asked for identification. A Sicilian pilot hired by Decatur replied, in Arabic, that the ship was a trading vessel from Malta. The freighter drifted closer. All was still; then someone on board the *Philadelphia* called out, *"Americani!"*

His cover blown, Decatur gave the order to board. American sailors

Commodore Edward Preble's fleet attacks Tripoli on August 3, 1804. The bombardment did not persuade the Tripolitan bashaw to release his American prisoners, and the Barbary War continued for another year.

swarmed onto the *Philadelphia*, cutting down the panicked pirates. As soon as the ship was cleared, they set it on fire and scrambled back onto the *Intrepid*. The fire reached the *Philadelphia*'s powder magazine, and the ship exploded. "The appearance of the ship was indeed magnificent," a sailor later wrote. "The flames,…ascending her rigging and masts, formed columns of fire."

The Barbary War continued until 1805. In another amazing adventure, former consul William Eaton led a force five hundred miles across the desert from Alexandria, Egypt, into Tripoli to take the city of Derna. His mostly mercenary army of Greeks, Arabs, and Turks included just eight American marines. Their exploits inspired the words of the Marine Hymn, "From the halls of Montezuma [Mexico] to the shores of Tripoli." (Both the U.S. Navy and the Marine Corps date their birth to the Barbary War.)

The United States and Algiers signed a peace treaty and the undeclared war came to an end. Just twenty-two years after the American Revolution ended, the new nation had proved that the world did not have to give in to piracy.

SOUTH AFRICA
RED SPEAR OF THE ZULUS

King Shaka was troubled. He had dreamed that he was dead. There had been one assassination attempt before. Many people had reason to hate him.

He was right to be worried. On the evening of September 24, 1828, he sat in his homestead, or kraal, and met with two tribesmen who had just returned from the frontier. Shaka was annoyed because they were late in arriving, and they trembled as they offered him valuable crane feathers and animal skins. The king often had his subjects put to death for small mistakes.

Suddenly Shaka's servant Mbopha beat the tribesmen away with a stick. Startled, Shaka rose from the ground—just as his half brothers Dingane and Mhlangana leaped over the kraal fence. First one, then the other, threw his spear at the king and struck him.

"What is the matter, my father's children?" Shaka cried. He stumbled and fell, and his attackers closed in.

Thus died Shaka, founder of the Zulu nation. In just eleven years, he had forged his people into a mighty nation of warriors, feared and respected throughout the land. Known as the "black Napoleon," he ruled over more territory and people than any king in southeastern Africa before him. But like many other conquerors, Shaka was a tyrant.

He was born in about 1787 in Natal, on the eastern shore of South Africa. The Zulus were a small clan, ruled over by Shaka's father, Senzangakhona. Like other Bantu-speaking peoples of eastern and southern Africa, they made their living herding cattle. They lived in kraals, groups of thatched huts surrounded by a fence. In the center of the kraal was a cattle pen. Cattle provided the Zulus with milk, meat, and hides, and were the main sign of wealth and status. Chiefs were known to be very wealthy

Shaka, king of the Zulus. In this nineteenth-century print, he is carrying a long Zulu throwing spear, called the assegai, and an ox-hide shield as tall as a man. When a British trader first met him in 1825, he reported that Shaka's "dress consists of monkey's skins, in three folds, from his waist to the knee, from which two cows' tails are suspended, as well as from each arm; around his head is a neat band of fur stuffed, in front of which is placed a tall feather, and on each side a variegated plume."

Women work outside a Zulu homestead, or kraal.
In 1800, each kraal was a self-sufficient community,
with its own grazing land and agricultural fields.

if they had so many cattle they could not recognize them all.

The people grew crops, too, such as corn, millet, sorghum, and sweet potatoes. Tending the fields was woman's work. Men had the more prestigious jobs of tending the cattle, hunting, and fighting. Young boys would take the cattle out to pasture to graze every morning and bring them back at noontime to be milked.

This way of life had remained stable for many centuries before Shaka was born, and was to remain so after his death. But he shook things up considerably while he was alive. Shaka had an unhappy childhood. His parents were not married when he was born, and his mother, Nandi, was of another, despised, clan. When the Zulu elders heard that she was pregnant, they insisted it could not be true. Nandi, they said, actually had an intestinal beetle—*iShaka*.

But it was a boy, not a beetle, and the Zulus were forced to take in the mother and son. Shaka was never really accepted. Like the other children, he was sent out at a young age to herd livestock. One day, one of the animals in the herd—Senzangakona's favorite—was killed by a dog, and Shaka was accused of being careless. He and his mother were banished from the clan. They went back to live with her people, who treated them very badly.

Shaka grew up to be angry and vengeful—and also immensely strong and intelligent. By the time he was a teenager, his abilities were obvious, and he was taken under the protection of Dingiswayo, chief of the neighboring Mthethwa. That is where Shaka learned to be a warrior.

At the time, the main weapon of the Zulus was a long throwing spear, the assegai. Shaka noticed that once the assegai was thrown, the warrior had no weapon for hand-to-hand combat. He designed a short broad stabbing spear to use at close range.

Soon he had the chance to show it off. Dingiswayo's warriors went to war against the Butelezi. When the armies met, a Butelezi warrior challenged the strongest Mthethwa warrior to single combat. Shaka stepped forward. But instead of throwing his long spear, he immediately broke into a run. His long ox-hide shield deflected the spear of his enemy as he charged forward, then he hooked his opponent's shield with his own. Jerking the shields to the left, he thrust his short spear into the man's heart. "*Ngadla!*" he shouted. "I have eaten!"

The short spear was just the first of Shaka's military innovations. He also discovered that if he took off his sandals and hardened his feet by

King Mpande, one of Shaka's successors, reviews his troops on a Zulu parade ground in 1847.

walking on thorns, he could run faster and with more agility. And he divided his army into three parts, with a central "chest" to meet the enemy straight on and two "horns" to envelop it from the sides. The warriors were drilled and drilled again until they formed an awesome fighting machine.

When Shaka's father died in 1816, Dingiswayo supported Shaka in overthrowing his half brother and becoming king himself. And after Dingiswayo was assassinated, Shaka took over his kingdom as well.

The new Zulu nation was formed along strictly military lines. Discipline was fierce. Warriors were divided into regiments by age and lived in special camps under their commanders. They could not marry until they were forty. Anyone found with a woman was killed. Anyone who showed pain was killed. Anyone who showed cowardice was killed. Anyone who displeased Shaka in any way was killed.

Finally Shaka set off on a terrible campaign of vengeance. His praise poem, which celebrates his victories, also reveals his ferocious personality:

> The young viper grows as it sits,
> Always in a great rage,
> With a shield on its knees....

He has not let them settle down, he keeps them in a state of excitement,
Those among the enemy and those at home.

Shaka began by destroying his mother's clan, which had treated him
so badly when he was young. Next he attacked the clan that had killed
Dingiswayo. Where he conquered, he was merciless—men, women, and
children were ruthlessly massacred. Captive young men became warriors,
and Shaka's army grew—to 10,000, then to 20,000 and 40,000.

 This terrible campaign has become known as the Mfecane, or "crush-
ing." As clans were attacked and driven from their lands, they in turn
attacked other clans and tried to take over their territory. A shock
wave of devastation spread across southeastern Africa. Europeans who

BATTLE DRESS

Preparing for battle was serious business for Shaka's army. Today we would say the warriors had to get "psyched" to fight. One of their prebattle rituals was to challenge one another in mock combat. First Shaka would call his warriors into the cattle enclosure at the center of the kraal. Then the warriors of each regiment would shout challenges to one another, working themselves up into a warlike frenzy.

To make the ritual convincing, the warriors would wear their ceremonial battle dress. Each regiment had a different uniform. One regiment might wear a headdress of otter and leopard skins with crane and ostrich feathers, for instance. Warriors also had white ox and cow tails hanging down their chests and backs, and oxtail fringes encircling their arms and legs. Their loincloths might be made from monkey tails or cowhide.

Men of high rank wore the same uniform as everyone else, but it was more elaborate. Shaka was known by the rare blue crane feather in his headband.

Warriors didn't wear all of these clothes into battle, of course. They needed to be able to move freely. But they did carry their impressive war shields, tall as a man and made of cattle hide. Each of Shaka's regiments could be identified by the color of its shield—all black, brown, or white, or black or brown with white spots. When the enemy saw these shields coming over a hill, they knew the Zulu army had arrived.

Utimuni, Shaka's nephew, in ceremonial battle dress, wearing an elaborate feathered headdress, ox and cow tails, and a loincloth made of monkey tails.

traveled across the land saw mile upon mile of scorched earth and whitening bones.

Under Shaka, the Zulu people never knew peace, only violence and killing. He was a great king and a magnificent warrior, but his only plan for his kingdom was war.

Toward the end of his reign, Shaka made friends with some British traders and even made them chiefs in his nation. The British had recently established trading posts in the area and Shaka recognized the importance of keeping peace with the white strangers. According to some sources, his last words to his assassins were a prophecy that, as soon as he died, the country would be overrun by "white people who will come up from the sea." Fifty years later, the British defeated his people in the Zulu War and broke up the Zulu nation.

After his death, Shaka the man became a myth. Majestic, cruel, brilliant, and ruthless, he is remembered as:

The voracious one of Senzangakhona,
Spear that is red even on the handle.

The national holiday of the Zulu people, Shaka Day, is celebrated on September 24, the anniversary of his assassination.

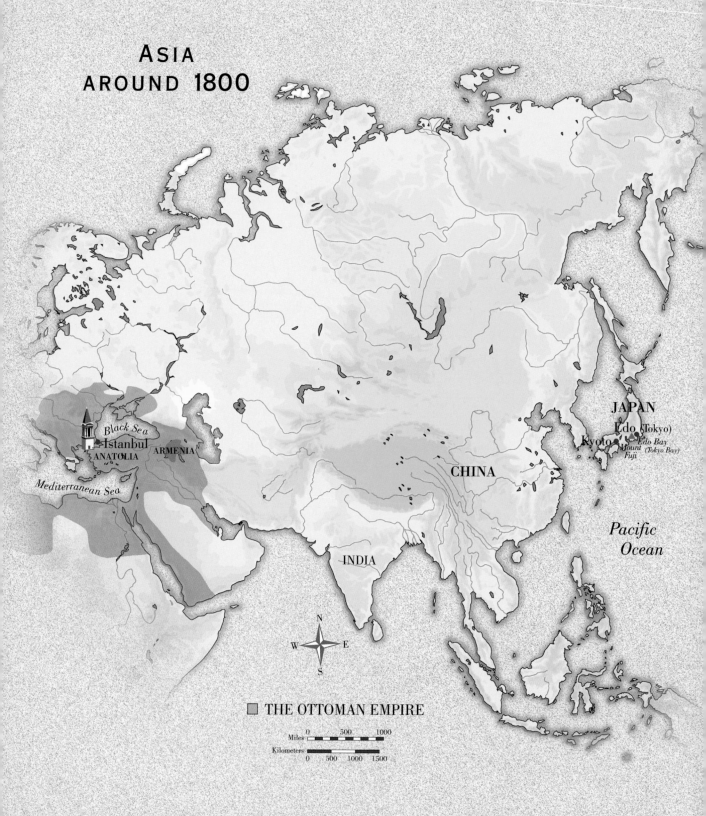

ASIA
AROUND 1800

Black Sea
Istanbul
ANATOLIA   ARMENIA
Mediterranean Sea

JAPAN
Edo (Tokyo)
Kyoto
Edo Bay
Mount (Tokyo Bay)
Fuji

CHINA

Pacific
Ocean

INDIA

N
W   E
S

☐ THE OTTOMAN EMPIRE

Miles 0   500   1000

Kilometers
       0   500   1000   1500

PART III
ASIA

In 1800, Asia had the most ancient civilizations in the world—in China, the Middle East, and India. Yet they were already in Europe's shadow. Despite its wealth, the vast Ottoman Empire was not keeping up with the technological advances of the West. In India and China, Britain had established trading centers that would allow it to extend its influence over both countries. Only the islands of Japan were able to take advantage of their isolation to keep their distance from Europe—and to keep their sovereignty.

As the world grew closer together, peoples who had long kept apart grew to know one another well for the first time.

IMPORTANT DATES
Turkey—The Reign of Abdul Hamid I
1774–1789

Japan—The Tokugawa Shogunate
1603–1867

TURKEY
THE OTTOMANS

Can you imagine a girl being captured by pirates and brought to an exotic land, where a fabulously wealthy king falls in love with her and makes her his bride (sort of)?

Sounds fantastic? It really happened to a girl named Aimee Dubucq de Rivery in 1784. She was sailing from France, where she had been at school, back home to the West Indies, when her ship was boarded by Barbary pirates. They took one look at the stunning blond-haired beauty and shipped her off to their boss, the dey of Algiers. The dey in turn thought she would be a perfect present for his ruler, the sultan.

That's how a twenty-one-year-old French girl ended up in the harem of Abdul Hamid I, the sultan of the Ottoman Empire, otherwise known as the Defender of the Faith, Lord of the Age, Sovereign of the Two Seas, Guardian of the Holy Places, and Shadow of God.

The Ottomans were a group of Islamic warriors from Anatolia (modern-day Turkey) who conquered the Christian city of Constantinople in 1453 and spread their empire over three continents. When Abdul Hamid I was sultan, he ruled over lands stretching from Bosnia and the Black Sea to the northern Mediterranean coast and down into North Africa. His territory included the modern countries of Bosnia, Serbia, Albania, Romania, Bulgaria, Greece, Georgia, Armenia, Turkey, Iraq, Syria, Lebanon, Israel, Egypt, Tunisia, and Algeria.

At the heart of the sultan's empire was the great city of Constantinople, which the Ottomans had renamed Istanbul. And at the heart of Istanbul was Topkapi, the palace of the sultan.

Topkapi was where Aimee was brought. First she would have passed

Sultan Selim III, who ruled the Ottoman Empire from 1789–1807, holds a formal reception in the second courtyard of Topkapi Palace. He is attended by a richly dressed assembly of ministers, ambassadors, agas (military commanders), and pashas (governors of provinces).

through the outer courtyard. In its five-thousand-square-foot expanse were the headquarters of everyone who served in the palace: merchants, gardeners, potters, bakers, weavers, guards, and soldiers with their horses.

It was a busy, bustling place, and one would have expected it to be very noisy.

But Topkapi was completely quiet. No one shouted, or sang, or whistled. The courtyard kept an almost religious solemnity. One visitor reported, "Anyone may enter the first court…but everything is so still, the Motion of the Fly might be heard in a manner…nay, the very horses seem to know where they are, and no doubt they are taught to tread softer than in the streets."

Through the Gate of Salutation lay the second courtyard. Here, where flowers bloomed and gazelles grazed on the lawns, the sultan governed from a gold throne. But Aimee would not have been allowed to dawdle. She would have been hurried through a third gate into the Abode of Bliss, the sultan's private household.

And there she stayed, a prisoner for life.

Like some one thousand other women, Aimee was a member of the sultan's harem. *Harīm* means "forbidden," and this area of the palace was forbidden to all men except the sultan and the sultan's eunuchs. It was a maze of small rooms, baths, courtyards, and gardens, and the women who lived there were never allowed to leave, not even to go to the sultan's quarters.

Aimee was really a slave, as was everyone else in his household. The other concubines were captives from Turkey, Armenia, or Abyssinia (Ethiopia). The eunuchs were Africans sold by Arab traders on the east coast of Africa. They were neutered when they were still boys and brought to Topkapi to guard the harem. Other female slaves were cooks, nursemaids, or maids.

Even the janissaries, the sultan's private army, were technically slaves. It was considered an honor to be a slave of the sultan. Some of the most powerful people in the empire—the head janissary, the head eunuch, the head concubine—were slaves.

The sultan fell in love with Aimee, and she became his head concubine (he had no wives). Her son, Mahmud II, became sultan in 1808. Whether she thought any of this was worth the freedom she gave up, we will never know.

Aimee came to the court of the sultan just when he began to realize the empire was old-fashioned. The janissaries, once unbeatable, were undisci-

*Women in a Turkish harem, as imagined by a
European artist in the nineteenth century*

SWORDS AND SOUP KETTLES

Cook. Soup man. Water carrier.

In the Ottoman Empire, these were not the names of workers in a kitchen or restaurant. They were titles of officers in the sultan's private army. Eating was so important to the janissaries that they honored their military commanders by giving them names having to do with food preparation and cleanup. Each regiment had its own huge copper kettle, in which the regimental stew was made. It was the most important symbol of the regiment. To lose a banner in battle was disgraceful. But to lose a kettle was catastrophic.

When the members of a regiment wanted to show their displeasure with the sultan, they overturned their cooking pot. That meant they were no longer accepting the sultan's food—or his authority.

Janissaries were fiercely loyal to their regiments. For centuries, the janissary troops were made up of eastern Europeans who were taken from their parents when they were boys, converted to Islam, and trained to become the sultan's warriors. Because these soldiers were not allowed to marry, the regiment was the only family they knew, and their loyalty to it was absolute.

By 1800, though, most of the janissaries were married and not nearly as loyal. With fewer wars to fight, they had become lazy and corrupt. Bands of soldiers wearing distinctive tall caps with soft white neck cloths

plined and weak. Their sabers were no match for modern European muskets and cannons. When Abdul Hamid's successor, Selim III, tried to bring the army up to date, however, he was resisted—and finally beaten—by the janissaries. It wasn't until Mahmud II became sultan that the army was finally modernized.

But by then, the Ottoman Empire was already in a long, slow decline. For the rest of the nineteenth century, it was chipped away as nationalist groups

Mahmud II, the son of Aimee Dubucq de Rivery, became sultan in 1808. It took him eighteen years of careful planning to finally get rid of the janissaries.

roamed through Istanbul and terrorized the populace. One of their favorite ways to make money was to set fire to houses and then demand payment to put the fires out.

Mahmud II knew it was time for the janissaries to go. But sultans before him had tried to get rid of the troops and failed. Secretly, Mahmud raised a new special army that would be loyal to him. Then he waited for the janissaries to find out about it and mutiny.

On June 14, 1826, the janissaries overturned their cooking pots. Immediately, Mahmud surrounded them with his soldiers and set fire to their section of Istanbul. Few of the trapped janissaries escaped the inferno.

Mahmud named the occasion the Auspicious (Happy) Event. The tyranny of the janissaries had ended.

among the Greeks, Bosnians, Egyptians, and other peoples revolted and established their own states. The empire's death knell came after World War I, when the winners, including England, France, and the United States, carved up the empire and parceled it out.

Then a great man, Kemal Atatürk, established Turkey as a modern republic. But that's another story.

JAPAN
A WORLD APART

In 1800, the Japanese stood alone. They had been cut off from outside influences for 165 years, and they wanted to keep it that way. After all, they thought, they were a divine people, with a divine ruler. What could the rest of the world have to offer?

At the head of Japanese society was the hereditary emperor. According to Shinto, the state religion, the emperor and his family were descended from the god and goddess who had created the islands of Japan. The emperor lived in splendor in his palace in Kyoto. But he had no power, and very little money. The absolute ruler of Japan was in fact the military dictator called the shogun. Since 1603, the shogun had always been a member of the Tokugawa family, descendants of the great general Tokugawa Ieyasu. Ieyasu and his predecessor, Hideyoshi, had subdued the dozens of nobles, called daimyo, who then ruled Japan, and had brought them under central control. After centuries of civil war, Japan was finally at peace.

Peace came at a price. The Tokugawa shoguns wanted to stop the clock—to keep Japan exactly as it had been in 1600. They did this by reinforcing a rigid social system, with the daimyo and their loyal samurai warriors at the top, peasants and artisans in the middle, and merchants at the bottom. (Merchants, it was believed, were inferior to other classes because they did not actually produce the products they sold.) All classes were subject to an intricate set of laws that governed everything from work and trade to marriage, clothes, and taxes.

The Tokugawa shoguns cut off Japan from the rest of the world. In 1635, the Edict of Closing declared that "Japanese ships are strictly forbidden to leave for foreign countries. No Japanese is permitted to go abroad. If any

Military hero Toyotomi Hideyoshi at the Siege of Inabayama in 1566. Hideyoshi's victories helped to unify Japan under stable military rule.

Japanese returns from overseas, after residing there, he must be put to death." Such strict measures were necessary, it was believed, to preserve Japanese culture and keep the peace. Japanese rulers had learned that Western trade meant Christian missionaries, and Christian missionaries meant civil unrest. Japanese who converted to Christianity might feel more loyal to God than to the shogun and the emperor. Since the emperor was the head not only of the country but of the state religion, such divided loyalties could tear the nation apart. In 1637, in fact, more than 20,000 Japanese Christians rebelled against the local daimyo and seized a castle. The rebellion was quashed only after the government intervened and nearly all the rebels were killed. The Tokugawa shoguns were determined that this would never happen again.

Isolated from the rest of the world, Japanese culture was free to develop on its own. That culture was marked by great beauty, refinement, and formality. Men and women wore long robes of silk or cotton bound by intricately constructed belts, or obis. The men's robes were plain, but the women's were decorated with colorful patterns and flowers and had immensely wide sleeves. Makeup was heavy and sophisticated, as one of the few Western visitors noted:

> The color with which they paint themselves is kept in little round porcelain boxes. With this they paint their lips.... If the paint is very thin, the lips appear red; but if it be laid on thick, they become of a violet hue, which here is considered as the greater beauty.
>
> That which chiefly distinguishes the married women from the single is their black teeth.... Some begin to make use of this ornament as soon as they are courted.

Women's hair was fluffed out and lacquered to form wings on the sides and a knot on top,

While men dressed plainly, fashionable Japanese women wore colorful kimonos, lacquered their hair, and applied heavy makeup.

ONE HUNDRED VIEWS OF MOUNT FUJI

The Japanese printmaker Hokusai (1760–1849) was the first to admit he was a late bloomer. "Until the age of seventy," he wrote, "nothing I drew was worthy of notice." Hokusai was apprenticed to a printmaker when he was fourteen. Like other artists (art was a thriving profession in Japan), he produced a variety of single prints and picture books on various subjects, particularly the *ukiyo*. But when he was seventy, he turned to the subject of Mount Fuji.

Why Mount Fuji? At 12,385 feet, the volcano is by far the highest mountain in Japan—its name means "peerless." Considered a sacred peak, it was climbed by many spiritual pilgrims in the nineteenth century. It is also called "deathless" and thought to confer immortality, or at least long life. Hokusai wanted to live longer in order to perfect his art: "At ninety [I hope] to see further into the underlying principles of things, so that at one hundred years I will have achieved a divine state in my art, and at one hundred and ten, every dot and stroke will be as though alive."

***Mount Fuji rises serenely into the clouds in Hokusai's* Fine Wind, Clear Morning.**

And so at age seventy Hokusai began the series of prints that would bring him artistic immortality: first the colored prints *Thirty-Six Views of Mount Fuji*, and then the black-and-white *One Hundred Views of Mount Fuji*. The prints contain an astonishing variety of scenes: geese flying, men fishing, a man cleaning a well, the volcano erupting, a dog howling at the moon, a spider building a web, soldiers cooking for an army, a goddess standing on a cloud. Behind, below, or above all these busy scenes rises Mount Fuji, the eternal mountain.

Hokusai did not live to see one hundred. He died at age ninety, in 1849. His last words were, "If only I could have just another ten years—another five years—then I could become a real artist."

stuck through with combs and ornaments. The front part of men's heads was shaved, and the remaining hair was bound up on top of the head with white string. Etiquette ruled everything: rules for eating, drinking, speaking, bowing, sitting, and walking were all strictly prescribed.

People living in such a formal society needed an escape hatch. And they found one, in the *ukiyo*, or "floating world." All cities had an area where one could find teahouses, bathhouses, theaters, and geisha houses. Pleasure was the order of the day: the *ukiyo* was all entertainment, all the time. Men

Actors in the first act of a Kabuki play based on a famous real-life tale of revenge. Kabuki was enjoyed for its dramatic plots, grandiose costumes, elaborate scenery, and stylized poses.

might gather in teahouses to read poetry to one another. The three-line haiku, evoking nature and the beauty of life, was especially popular by the end of the eighteenth century. Or they might listen to a geisha sing and play the samisen. Or they might go to a splendid Kabuki play. Kabuki, with its exciting stories and brilliant pageantry, was a major art form by 1800.

In 1800, it must have seemed as if this way of life would never end. But there were already signs of change. Merchants, presumably on the lowest level of society, were often more prosperous than the higher-caste daimyo. The samurai, the daimyo's loyal warriors, had actually lost their jobs with the coming of peace and were forced to educate themselves for other professions. Now they were no longer warriors but civil servants. Clearly, life had not stood still for the past two centuries after all.

And despite the embargo on foreign goods, the shogun and his counselors were aware of the Industrial Revolution in Europe and the United States. There seemed an ever-increasing possibility that Japan, for all its knowledge and sophistication, was falling behind.

So when Commodore Matthew Perry of the United States Navy steamed into Edo (now Tokyo) Bay on July 8, 1853, asking for trade privileges, the government had to consider his offer. Ultimately, the United States did reach an agreement with Japan to open up the islands to the rest of the world. Agreements with the British, the Dutch, and the Russians followed. Just fifteen years later, the 250-year-old Tokugawa shogunate was overthrown, and Japan began the process of modernization.

But in 1800, Japan was still in a dream of its own making. Who could tell what enormous changes lay ahead?

AUSTRALIA
AROUND 1800

TIMOR

Coral Sea

Great Sandy Desert

Gibson Desert

Great Victoria Desert

I n d i a n   O c e a n

N
W   E
S

Sydney
Botany Bay

Melbourne

Tasman Sea

VAN DIEMEN'S LAND
(TASMANIA)

Miles   0   200   500
Kilometers 0   400   800

PART IV

AUSTRALIA

To most people in 1800, Australia seemed like the end of the world. Larger than an island and smaller than other continents, it had a vast, nearly empty interior rimmed by fertile shores. Australia's native peoples, the Aborigines, had inhabited this land undisturbed for 50,000 years. Their ancient way of life ended in 1787. That was when the British decided to colonize the land.

IMPORTANT DATES
Australia—Prison Colony
1788–1864

AUSTRALIA
A PRISON CONTINENT

On January 18, 1788, a fleet of ships sailed into Australia's Botany Bay. The 1,030 people on the eleven ships had been at sea for 252 days. The new land they gazed out on was flat and desolate, with miles of bushy scrub and gray eucalyptus trees. It looked most uninviting. Yet these people would have to farm this sandy soil and somehow make it grow crops. For they were British convicts. All of Australia was to be their prison.

Britain was in desperate need of prisons in the late eighteenth century. Before the American Revolution, it had shipped many of its convicts to the colonies. But after the peace settlement in 1783, it had to find a new solution.

Captain James Cook had claimed Australia for Britain in 1770. His botanist, Joseph Banks, sent back reports of a bizarre land filled with even more bizarre creatures: kangaroos, koalas, and wombats, anteating echidnas and amphibious duck-billed platypuses. The land was fertile, Banks reported, and nearly empty.

Oh, there were people living on the land, but not enough to worry about. There were only about 300,000 Aborigines on the whole continent in 1788— the equivalent of one person for every ten miles.

When the convicts landed, some of the native people gathered on the beach to watch the strange white foreigners in their white-sailed boats. A few shook their spears and shouted, *"Warra warra!"* ("Go away!")

But the British were there to stay. The first two years they nearly starved; at one point some of them were reduced to eating seaweed they had scraped off rocks and boiled. Then ships brought more convicts and more supplies. Soon the colony was self-supporting.

Only the most rebellious convicts spent time in actual prisons when they

The first British settlers in Australia were convicts, like the members of this labor gang in Sydney in the early 1800s. Put to work building towns and roads for the government, convicts often died under the brutal discipline and grueling heat. Some of these laborers are wearing leg irons.

got to Australia. The rest were put to work by the government or rented out to farmers as help. Most of the convicts were not hardened criminals. They had been transported for petty thievery of goods such as tools, clothes, or

DREAMTIME

Australia is an old land. Its dry, dusty hills were once mountains; its deserts were once forests. Aborigines have been living there for nearly as long as the land has existed. It is their land. Not because they own it—Aborigines do not think of land as property, to be owned by individuals. But according to Aboriginal beliefs, the land is the source of all life and meaning.

For Aborigines, every rock, stream, and bush has sacred importance. They were all created by the Ancestors during the Dreamtime. That was when the Ancestors came up out of the earth, fashioned themselves from clay, and walked over the continent. As they walked, they sang—and their songs created the world. They sang of rocks—and the rocks existed. They sang of plants—and

An Aboriginal painting, done on eucalyptus bark, of a kangaroo and hunter

food. Their sentences were for seven or fourteen years. Punishment for any infraction of the rules was severe. The preferred punishment was flogging: fifty or even one hundred lashes of the cat-o'-nine-tails was common.

*Before the coming of Europeans, Aborigines roamed a
vast landscape of craggy hills, open grassland, and desert.
They ranged as groups throughout vast tribal territories, where
they hunted, fished, and gathered plants for food.*

the plants existed. They sang of snakes and lizards and wallabies, and
suddenly snakes slithered, lizards crawled, and wallabies jumped
across the land.

The paths along which the Ancestors walked are called the songlines.
Australia is crisscrossed by thousands of songlines, which Aborigines
follow on "walkabouts." Reciting traditional songs, they make the land
come alive—and re-create the creation of the Ancestors.

After they got their "ticket of leave," or probation, former convicts could
return to England if they wanted to. Few ever did. No matter how hard life
in Australia might be, it was better than being an unskilled worker—in a

factory or on a farm—in England. And skilled workers—blacksmiths, carpenters, cobblers, coopers—had it made in the new land. Australia was a land of opportunity.

In the meantime, the convicts had to live with the System, as it was called. Because for most their prison had no actual bars, many tried to run away. These "bolters" were often found weeks later in the Australian bush, dazed and starving, or already dead.

Others tried to escape by sea. Mary Bryant, who had been transported for stealing a cloak, made her escape in 1791 with her husband, their two young children, and seven other adults. They sailed a stolen boat 3,250 miles from Sydney to Timor, an island in Indonesia—the first people since Captain Cook to make the voyage. Menaced by fierce storms and warlike cannibals, they survived by eating edible palms, fish, and sea turtles. Incredibly, they were all alive when they reached Timor—where the Dutch governor turned them over to the English. Mary was eventually shipped back to England. She was about to be transported again to Australia when she was pardoned by the king. "The Girl from Botany Bay," as Mary was known, became an inspiration to other would-be bolters.

At first, escaped convicts who "ranged the bush" formed gangs and hunted kangaroos. Later, when big sheep farms were established, they stole sheep. Most of the bushrangers were vicious thugs. But since some stole from the rich and sold to the poor, they earned a reputation as Australian Robin Hoods.

One local hero was Matthew Brady, who had been transported for stealing bacon, butter, and rice. After he escaped in 1824, he and his gang ranged the bush in Tasmania, then called Van Diemen's Land. Although the government set up an intensive manhunt, the gang was aided by convict servants across the land, who would hide them and give them guns. A sentimental man, Brady never allowed his gang to hurt women. When Brady was finally caught, women brought him flowers, cakes, and letters in prison. But his fate was sealed, and he was hanged as an example to others.

The island continent of Australia is home to a number of creatures found nowhere else on earth, such as the kangaroo. Prized for its venison-like meat and tough hide, the kangaroo was hunted by Aborigine and settler alike.

The last convict was sent to Australia in 1864. By then, sheep, gold, and oil had made the country rich. But despite their new respectability, many Australians remained rebels at heart. The most famous bushranger of all was Ned Kelly (1855–1880). He and his gang ranged the bush for several years, stealing horses and defying the authorities. When he was finally cornered by the police, Kelly faced the shoot-out wearing home-made metal armor under his coat and a bucket on his head. Today he is Australia's most famous folk hero.

The legend of the bushranger lives on.

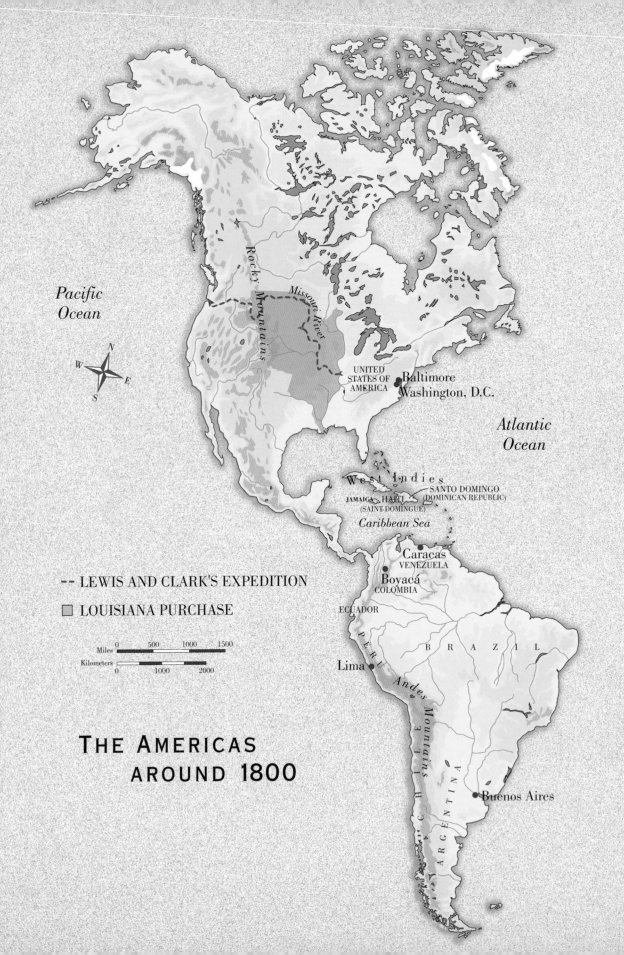

*Pacific
Ocean*

Rocky Mountains

Missouri River

UNITED
STATES OF
AMERICA

●Baltimore
Washington, D.C.

*Atlantic
Ocean*

West Indies

SANTO DOMINGO
(DOMINICAN REPUBLIC)

JAMAICA HAITI
(SAINT-DOMINGUE)

Caribbean Sea

●Caracas
VENEZUELA

●Boyacá
COLOMBIA

ECUADOR

B R A Z I L

Andes Mountains

Lima●

●Buenos Aires

-- LEWIS AND CLARK'S EXPEDITION

☐ LOUISIANA PURCHASE

Miles 0   500   1000   1500

Kilometers 0   1000   2000

The Americas
around 1800

PART V

THE AMERICAS

Around 1800, the Americas were reborn. Colonized by Europe nearly three hundred years before, they had been ruled from overseas ever since. Now they were ready for freedom. First, in 1776, the thirteen North American colonies rebelled against England. Then, in 1791, the West Indian colony of Saint-Domingue (Haiti) rebelled against France. And from 1811 to 1824, Spanish colonies from North to South America rebelled against Spain.

While most of Africa and Asia would be dominated by Europe for the next century and a half, these new American countries were on their own. The hard work of becoming successful independent nations had just begun.

IMPORTANT DATES

The American Revolution
1776–1783

The Haitian Revolution
1791–1804

Revolution in Spanish America
1810–1824

THE UNITED STATES
A BOLD NEW EXPERIMENT

The United States at the start of the nineteenth century was still a bold experiment. No one knew for sure whether it was actually going to work. Just twenty-five years earlier, the ringing words of the Declaration of Independence had declared for the first time in the history of human societies that "all men are created equal" and that they have the right to "life, liberty, and the pursuit of happiness." In 1788, a new constitution described how a government based on these principles would work. The new republic had neither a king nor a dictator, but was run by representatives of those citizens who were eligible to vote.

The United States in 1800 was by no means a perfect democracy. Large numbers of Americans—women, Native Americans, most African Americans, and men who did not own land—could not vote. (Suffrage would be extended slowly to various groups over the next 150 years.) But the United States *had* shown the rest of the world that it was possible for a people to choose their own form of government.

Even more important, Americans proved that a republican form of government could run smoothly. When Thomas Jefferson was elected president in 1800, power passed from the Federalist Party of George Washington and John Adams to Jefferson's Republican Party. Some historians call Jefferson's inauguration the most important in American history. One eyewitness, Margaret Bayard Smith, knew the significance of what she had seen. On March 4, 1801, she wrote:

> I have this morning witnessed one of the most interesting scenes a
> free people can ever witness. The changes of administration, which

A view of New York City at Wall and Water Streets, around 1797.
At the start of the nineteenth century, the United States was still a
nation of farms and small towns, and even New York, the largest city,
had no more than 80,000 inhabitants. The building on the left is the
Tontine Coffee House, the forerunner of the New York Stock Exchange.
Investment and trade helped fund the growth of the new nation.

in every government and in every age have most generally been epochs
of confusion, villainy and bloodshed, in this our happy country take
place without any species of distraction or disorder.

As Europe erupted in the violence of the French Revolution and then
the Napoleonic Wars, America's first presidents, George Washington,

American sailors are impressed into the British navy in 1807.
The kidnapping of Americans on the high seas helped spark the
War of 1812 between Great Britain and the United States.

John Adams, and Thomas Jefferson, tried to steer the country clear of
involvement. But the Napoleonic Wars ended up being a worldwide conflict.
Britain and France each tried to cut off American trade with the other.
Both seized American ships, and Britain went even further: it kidnapped
American sailors to serve in the British navy.

"War hawks" in Congress demanded action, and in 1812 President James

Madison gave in and declared war against Great Britain. Luckily, the war didn't last very long. By December 1814, it was over, and the relationship between the mother country and her former colonies quickly improved. They soon became allies. From the War of 1812, the United States gained self-respect and a new national anthem: "The Star-Spangled Banner," written by Francis Scott Key during the British bombardment of Baltimore in 1814.

So the first years of the nineteenth century were good to the fledgling nation. Revolution and wars raged on around it, while the United States stubbornly held to the course of nation building. By 1803, the size of the new nation had doubled. It was all due to a very lucky real estate deal.

Across the ocean in Europe, Napoleon Bonaparte had to raise some money—fast. He was about to embark on another round of wars and needed to finance them. So he offered the whole of the Louisiana Territory—829,000 square miles—to President Thomas Jefferson for the bargain-basement sum of fifteen million dollars. That came out to just four cents an acre.

Naturally, the United States snapped it up. The Louisiana Purchase was a triumph for the new republic. It covered most of the territory that later became Iowa, Kansas, Arkansas, Missouri, North Dakota, South Dakota, Nebraska, Wyoming, Minnesota, Oklahoma, Montana, Colorado, and Louisiana.

Even before the treaty was signed, Jefferson chose his personal secretary, Meriwether Lewis, and Lewis's friend William Clark to explore the western territory. He wanted them to find out about the climate, wildlife, and resources of the land. Even more important, Lewis and Clark were instructed to make friends with the region's Native Americans.

The Corps of Discovery set off up the Missouri River in May 1804 with a force of about fifty men. By the time they returned, almost two-and-a-half years later, they had traveled more than seven thousand miles and described 122 species of animals and 178 species of plants new to science, and met 24 unknown Native American tribes. They had gone

INDIAN TERRITORY

The land that Lewis and Clark explored was, of course, already occupied—by Native Americans. The corps met nearly fifty different Indian tribes on its journey. President Jefferson wanted Meriwether Lewis to assure the Native Americans of "our wish to be neighborly, friendly, and useful to them." Jefferson considered them important trading partners. He also wanted them to be the allies of the United States against the British and Spanish.

Lewis tried to impress the native peoples by distributing gifts: clothing, mirrors, razors, needles, tomahawks, guns, and whiskey. He handed friendship medals to the chiefs, with an image of Jefferson on one side and two hands clasping on the other. They were invited to visit the "great father" in Washington, D.C. A few chiefs actually made the long journey.

Relations between members of the corps and Native Americans were mostly friendly on both sides. But the friendships did not last. In the course of the century, hunters, trappers, and settlers moved west and took over the Indians' hereditary lands. Many Indian populations were devastated by disease and alcoholism. For Native Americans, the Lewis and Clark Expedition signaled the beginning of the end of their traditional way of life.

down raging rivers, crossed icy mountains, and fought fierce grizzly bears. Only one member of the corps lost his life—to appendicitis.

By November 7, 1805, Lewis and Clark had crossed the Rocky Mountains and reached their goal. Lewis wrote in his journal, "Great joy in camp.

Sacagawea guides Lewis and Clark through the Rocky Mountains in this painting by N.C. Wyeth, 1940. She was of invaluable help to the expedition.

So it is ironic that the expedition member we remember best today was a Shoshoni woman. Sacagawea accompanied her husband, a French trader, on the long journey. This eighteen-year-old girl with a newborn baby on her back was one of the most useful members of the corps. She knew how to gather essential roots, greens, and berries, and how to fight—and avoid—fierce grizzly bears. When the group reached the Rocky Mountains, she acted as interpreter to the Shoshoni tribe and helped the corps purchase horses to take them across the mountains. In their journals, Lewis and Clark both praised her courage and stamina. She must have been adventurous, too. When the corps reached the Pacific Ocean, Sacagawea insisted that she accompany the others to see a whale that had been beached on the shore. She had come a long way to see the big waters, she said, and she would not be left behind.

We are in view of the ocean—this great Pacific Ocean which we have been so long anxious to see." The United States did not yet reach from "sea to shining sea" (the Oregon Territory would be added in 1846) but already it had staked its claim to the continent.

HAITI
NIGHT OF FIRE

On the night of August 22, 1791, Haiti burned. Flames climbed from plantation to mountain, from sugarcane field to cotton shed. By daybreak, the news had spread: the slaves had rebelled.

In the 1780s, Haiti was a French colony of great wealth, called Saint-Domingue. Its plantations grew half of Europe's sugar, cotton, and coffee. Every year, shiploads of Africans were imported to work in the fields: 8,000 in 1720; 27,000 in 1786; and 40,000 in 1787. On the eve of the French Revolution, there were 500,000 slaves in Haiti and only 70,000 free whites, blacks, and mulattos. The colony had the largest percentage of blacks of any country in the Americas.

So many blacks had to be imported because conditions were so horrific that they kept dying. Field slaves were worked eighteen hours a day in the broiling

Slaves on Saint-Domingue fight French troops. The 1791 Haitian revolt was the most successful slave rebellion in history.

tropical heat and nearly starved. To enforce obedience, masters used every brutality imaginable: whipping, burning, mutilation, torture of various kinds. The level of cruelty on the plantations was almost unimaginable.

Household slaves often had it better. One intelligent little boy named Toussaint had a kind master who encouraged him not only to read and write but to study history, religion, and military science. When he was a teenager, Toussaint later recalled, he saw a man burned alive for trying to poison his master. He never forgot the sight.

Haitians of all classes heard about the French Revolution in 1789. White colonists were inspired to ask for the right to form their own government. They got it. But France's new National Assembly refused to grant freedom to the slaves. So in 1791, Haiti's slaves began a revolution of their own. They marched from plantation to plantation, burning homes, mills, and sugarcane fields, murdering whites and mulattos, and destroying everything in their path.

At first Toussaint held back and watched. By now, he was a middle-aged man, the respected steward of his master's household. Despite being small and ugly, Toussaint had great natural authority and intelligence. When he did decide to join the rebels, he first made sure that his own family and the family of his master escaped to the Dominican Republic (then Santo Domingo).

Then he took over the rebel mobs and forged them into an army. With the knowledge he had gained from reading military books, he drilled a small group of men. He taught them how to use the guns they took from defeated French troops and how to fire cannons without blowing themselves up.

At first, he fought on the side of the Spanish and British against the French. When the French revolutionary government finally abolished slavery, Toussaint and his troops immediately switched sides and began fighting on the side of the French. All foreigners were driven from the land.

Reconstruction would be hard. War had devastated Haiti; nearly a third of the populace had died or fled the country. Toussaint envisioned a republic where blacks and whites were free and equal, with a thriving economy, equitable law courts, and education for all. On July 7, 1801, he was named governor for life.

But Toussaint's dream was not to be. By 1801, Napoleon was in power in France, and Napoleon was no abolitionist. He wanted to bring Haiti back under French control and to reinstitute slavery.

He sent a force of 35,000 men to recapture the island. His men kidnapped Toussaint and sent him to France, where he died of exposure in a cold, dank dungeon. But Toussaint's troops fought on, and 15,000 Frenchmen eventually lost their lives. Finally, defeated by yellow fever and ex-slaves, Napoleon withdrew his troops.

Haiti declared its independence on January 1, 1804. It was the first country to outlaw slavery in the New World.

VOODOO

Night after night in the slave colony of Saint-Domingue, there was drumming in the hills. Escaped slaves, called Maroons, were chanting and dancing in the religious rituals of voodoo. Others, listening on plantations, danced in the dark. It was the sound of slave rebellion.

West African slaves had brought their religious beliefs with them to the New World. Although slaves were baptized by the Roman Catholic Church when they first arrived in Haiti, they continued practicing their old religions in secret. Voodoo, which means "spirit" in an African language, is a West Indian fusion of Yoruba, Fon, Congo, and other West African religions.

There are thousands of gods, or *loa*, in voodoo. Some are derived from African gods and others resemble Roman Catholic saints. Oshun, the goddess of love, is fused with the Virgin Mary. Damballa, the snake god, is identified with Saint Patrick. In voodoo rituals, people make contact with the *loas* and offer them animal sacrifices. They believe the *loas* provide health, good fortune, and protection from evil spirits.

French slave owners feared voodoo, which they suspected of uniting slaves from plantation to plantation. They were right. On August 14, 1791, the voodoo priest Boukman secretly gathered dozens of slaves in the woods and planned a rebellion. In a frenzied ceremony, they chanted revenge against the white slave owners. A week later—on the Night of Fire—Haiti went up in flames.

Twentieth-century Haitians participate in a voodoo ceremony.

VENEZUELA
FIGHTING FOR FREEDOM

One sunny day in 1800, Prince Ferdinand of Spain was playing racquetball with a teenage visitor. The contest was just heating up when–*whack!*–the visitor's racket knocked the prince's hat off his head.

The prince knew it was an accident. But he still demanded an apology. The teenager refused. "If I ever choose to strike you on purpose, you will know it," he said haughtily.

The proud visitor was a wealthy Venezuelan named Simón Bolívar (1783–1830). Twenty years later, he did strike at the prince (by then the king) on purpose. He led a South American rebellion against Spain.

Like most of South and Central America, Venezuela was a Spanish colony in 1800. The land had been under Spanish control since the Spanish conquistadors had seized it from the Indians in the early sixteenth century. From the beginning, the colonies had a rigid social structure. At the top were the *Peninsulars*, Spaniards who had been born in Spain, followed by the Creoles, people of Spanish ancestry. Further down the social ladder were the mestizos, people of mixed Spanish and

Simón Bolívar is revered as the "Liberator" of South America.

Simón Bolívar marches in triumph through the streets of Caracas after defeating the Spanish.

Indian blood, and then the Indian laborers and, finally, the African slaves.

Although the Spanish colonists had lived in Venezuela for three hundred years, most decisions about the colony were made on the other side of the Atlantic Ocean. Creoles especially disliked their lack of power. Like the Bolívar family, they were usually wealthy landowners who resented having to pay taxes to an absent government. When trading ships first brought news of the French Revolution, young Creoles were inspired by the ideas of freedom and liberty.

So young Bolívar grew up listening to talk of revolution. Napoleon Bonaparte was his hero. Later, when Bonaparte made himself emperor, Bolívar, like so many others, became disillusioned with the egotistical dictator. But he did not lose his idealism.

Bolívar resolved to liberate his country. At age twenty, he declared, "I will not rest, not in body or soul, until I have broken the chains of Spain."

Napoleon actually provided Venezuelans with an excuse to rebel. In 1808, he conquered Spain and placed his brother Joseph on the throne. People in the colony refused to recognize the "new" Spanish government—and on July 5, 1811, Venezuela declared its independence from Spain.

The war that followed was long and extraordinarily brutal. It was actually a civil war, because Venezuela itself was divided. The upper classes were usually royalist, on the side of Spain. The lower classes had mixed loyalties.

THE OTHER LIBERATOR

There is not just one famous South American liberator, but two. The other was José de San Martín (1778–1850), who freed Argentina, Chile, and part of Peru from Spanish rule. San Martín was as different as possible from Simón Bolívar. Bolívar was dramatic and emotional. San Martín was quiet and reserved. Bolívar was interested in political power. San Martín was not. A soldier above all, he only wanted to win battles.

Although San Martín was born in Argentina, he actually fought for Spain against Napoleon in Europe. Twenty-two years in the Spanish army gave him the experience he needed to fight for Argentina. When San Martín returned to Buenos Aires in 1812, the leaders of the new Argentine army put him in charge of a cavalry regiment—and then the entire army.

Like Bolívar's army, San Martín's also crossed the Andes. He wanted to invade Chile from Argentina. But unlike impulsive Bolívar, who decided to attempt the dangerous crossing at the last moment, San Martín prepared his army for a whole year. Women sewed uniforms and made shoes. A factory made guns, bullets, and swords. San Martín drilled his troops and prepared them for the 12,000 foot-high crossing.

He cheered his men over the mountains—and they came down the other side to drive the Spanish out of Chile. He went on to enter Peru and free the city of Lima. But the Spanish in Peru outnumbered San Martín's forces two to one. It was time to bring in another army.

In July 1822, José San Martín went to Ecuador to meet with Simón

Following a series of early defeats, Bolívar and his army of peasants were triumphant at last. He swept through Spanish-controlled territory, capturing town after town. From each one, he sent a dispatch, proclaiming it had been liberated. By the time he marched into the capital, Caracas, he was known as El Libertador (the Liberator).

But his triumphs did not last. The royalists did not give up so quickly.

Bolívar. They talked by themselves in a small room, and no one has ever known what they said to each other. But after the meeting, San Martín left the building without saying a word—and resigned from the independence movement. From then on, it was all up to Bolívar.

Probably San Martín realized that he could never work with the

volatile and ambitious Bolívar. He was tired after thirty years of combat, and willing to pass the leadership of the revolution to someone else. But Argentineans did not understand. After San Martín had led them to independence, they rejected him. San Martín lived the rest of his life in France with his daughter and grandchildren. Not until 1880 would the Argentineans forgive their hero—and bring his body home.

José de San Martín fought for the freedom of Argentina, Chile, and Peru.

The deadliest of the royalists was actually a Venezuelan cowboy—an *illaneros*—named José Tomas Boves. Boves and his forces would storm into villages and massacre everyone—men, women, and children. People called his forces the Legion of Hell.

In six years, one-quarter of the people of Venezuela lost their lives. Bolívar retreated to the Caribbean island of Jamaica to consider what to do next. Meanwhile, over in Europe, Napoleon was finally defeated, and the Spanish king turned his attention to the rebels in South America. Determined to crush the revolution, his troops massacred villagers and burned cities.

It was then that Bolívar conceived his most daring plan. He decided to lead his men over the Andes Mountains and attack the Spanish troops in what is now Colombia. "Where a goat can go an army can go," he declared. No one had ever crossed mountains so high—the Andes soar to 12,000 feet—with a large army.

The narrow mountain pass was treacherous, and men and animals slipped off its icy slopes to be lost forever. When the surviving troops finally stumbled down the mountain in August 1819, they surprised the Spanish at Boyacá and defeated them.

Colombia was free of Spanish rule. By 1822, Bolívar had beaten the Spanish in Venezuela and Ecuador, too. The Argentine revolutionary, José de San Martín had defeated them in Argentina and Chile. When Bolívar invaded Peru, it became independent, too.

Bolívar's dream was to unite all of South America (except for Portuguese-speaking Brazil) into one nation, like the United States. As a first step, he united Venezuela, Colombia, and Ecuador into the republic of Gran Colombia and made himself president. But the union soon dissolved as the countries began to quarrel and fight with one another.

Bolívar decided it was hopeless. "Those who fight in South America's revolution," he declared, "only plow the sea." He resigned as president and died soon thereafter, at the age of forty-seven.

WORLD EVENTS AROUND 1800

1733—John Kay invents flying shuttle

1764—James Hargreaves invents spinning jenny

1774—Johann Wolfgang von Goethe publishes *The Sorrows of Young Werther*

1776—Declaration of Independence written; American Revolution begins

1783—American Revolution ends

1788—First British convicts land in Australia

1789—French Revolution begins; adoption of Declaration of the Rights of Man and Citizen

1791—Haitian Revolution begins

1792—France declares war on Austria

1793—Louis XVI and Queen Marie Antoinette guillotined in Paris

1800—Napoleon elected first consul of France

1801—Barbary War begins

1803—President Jefferson buys Louisiana Territory from France
    —Ludwig van Beethoven publishes Third Symphony, the *Eroica*

1804—Napoleon crowns himself emperor of the French
    —Haitian Revolution ends
    —Lewis and Clark Expedition begins
    —First steam locomotive runs on rails in England

1805—Napoleon defeats combined Russian and Austrian armies at Austerlitz
    —Barbary War ends

1806—Lewis and Clark Expedition ends

1807—Britain abolishes slave trade

1808—The United States abolishes slave trade
    —Mahmud II becomes sultan of the Ottoman Empire

1811—Venezuela declares independence from Spain

1812—Napoleon invades Russia

1815—Napoleon defeated at Battle of Waterloo; Congress of Vienna concludes

1816—Shaka becomes king of the Zulus

1817—José de San Martín crosses the Andes and defeats the Spanish in Chile

1819—Simón Bolívar crosses the Andes and defeats the Spanish in Colombia

1821—Napoleon dies

1824—Bolívar wins final battle for South American independence in Peru

1826—Sultan Mahmud II destroys janissaries

1828—Shaka assassinated

1833—Britain abolishes slavery throughout its empire

1851—Crystal Palace Exhibition in London

1853—Commodore Matthew Perry opens Japan

GLOSSARY

abolitionist A person who tries to get rid of slavery.

Aborigines The native peoples of Australia.

assegai The long throwing spear of the Zulus.

Barbary Coast European name for the northern coast of Africa.

breeches Short pants reaching just below the knee.

bushranger An Australian outlaw living in the bush.

clan A group of families united by the belief that they are all descended from the same ancestor.

cooper A person who makes wooden casks.

daimyo A Japanese nobleman.

dey A ruling official of the Ottoman Empire in North Africa.

geisha A Japanese woman trained to entertain a group of men.

harem The secluded part of a traditional Muslim household, where the women live.

illaneros A Venezuelan cowboy.

Industrial Revolution Social and economic changes brought by the introduction of power-driven machinery in Europe and the United States in the late eighteenth and early nineteenth centuries.

janissaries Members of an elite corps of Turkish troops in the Ottoman Empire, who made up the sultan's private army.

Kabuki A traditional, highly stylized Japanese drama with singing and dancing.

kraal In southern Africa, a village surrounded by a fence.

liberal Someone who supports individual freedom and social reform.

millet A grain used for food.

myth A popular belief or tradition that grows up around a person, an institution, or an idea.

Ottomans The rulers of Turkey and much of Asia, Europe, and Africa from the thirteenth century until 1918.

pantaloons Close-fitting trousers with a strap passing under the foot.

radical Someone who supports extreme measures to either change or retain a government or political policy.

ritual A ceremonial act.

Romanticism A literary, artistic, and philosophical movement starting in the late eighteenth century that emphasized emotion and the power of the imagination.

samisen A three-stringed Japanese musical instrument.

samurai A specially trained warrior loyal to a daimyo, or Japanese noble.

shogun A military ruler of Japan.

sorghum A cornlike grain.

subsistence The minimum amount of food and shelter necessary to keep people alive.

sultan The hereditary ruler of the Ottoman Empire.

Third Estate The peasant and middle classes in France before the French Revolution in 1789. The First Estate was the clergy; the Second Estate was the nobility.

FOR FURTHER READING

Baker, Nina Brown. *He Wouldn't Be King: The Story of Simon Bolivar.* New York: Vanguard Press, 1941.

Blumberg, Rhoda. *Commodore Perry in the Land of the Shogun.* New York: Lothrop, Lee, and Shepard, 1985.

————. *The Incredible Journey of Lewis and Clark.* New York: Lothrop, Lee, and Shepard, 1987.

————. *What's the Deal? Jefferson, Napoleon, and the Louisiana Purchase.* Washington, D.C.: National Geographic Society, 1998.

Cairns, Trevor. *Power for the People.* Minneapolis: Lerner, 1980.

Chamberlin, E. R. *Everyday Life: The Nineteenth Century.* London: McDonald & Co., 1983.

Clare, John D., ed. *The Industrial Revolution.* San Diego: Lucent Books, 1998.

Corrick, James A. *The Industrial Revolution.* San Diego: Lucent Books, 1998.

Crane, William D. *James Watt: The Man Who Transformed the World.* New York: Julian Messner, 1963.

Faber, Doris, and Harold Faber. *The Birth of a Nation: The Early Years of the United States.* New York: Scribner's, 1989.

Gilbert, Adrian. *The French Revolution.* New York: Thomson Learning, 1995.

Gilford, Henry. *Voodoo: Its Origins and Practices.* New York: Franklin Watts, 1976.

Hall, Eleanor J. *Life among the Samurai.* San Diego: Lucent Books, 1999.

Haskins, James, and Kathleen Benson. *Bound for America: The Forced Migration of Africans to the New World.* New York: Lothrop, Lee, and Shepard, 1999.

Hoobler, Dorothy, and Thomas Hoobler. *South American Portraits.* Austin: Raintree Steck-Vaughn, 1994.

Jacobs, William Jay. *Great Lives: World Government.* New York: Scribner's, 1992.

Killingray, David. *The Transatlantic Slave Trade.* London: B. T. Batsford, 1987.

Marrin, Albert. *Napoleon and the Napoleonic Wars.* New York: Viking, 1991.

McGuire, Leslie. *Napoleon.* New York: Chelsea House, 1986.

Meltzer, Milton. *Slavery II: From the Renaissance to Today.* Chicago: Cowles Book Company, 1972.

Mitchison, Naomi. *African Heroes.* New York: Farrar, Straus, and Giroux, 1968.

Morris, Jeffrey. *The Jefferson Way.* Minneapolis: Lerner, 1994.

Roberson, John R. *Japan: From Shogun to Sony, 1543–1984.* New York: Atheneum, 1985.

Roop, Peter, and Connie Roop, eds. *Off the Map: The Journals of Lewis and Clark.* New York: Walker and Company, 1993.

Sheehan, Sean. *Turkey.* New York: Marshall Cavendish, 1993.

Spencer, William. *The Land and People of Turkey.* New York: J. B. Lippincott, 1990.

Stanley, Diane, and Peter Vennema. *Shaka: King of the Zulus.* New York: Morrow, 1988.

Stein, R. Conrad. *The Story of the Barbary Pirates.* Chicago: Children's Press, 1982.

St. George, Judith. *Sacagawea.* New York: Putnam, 1997.

Tames, Richard. *Ludwig van Beethoven.* New York: Franklin Watts, 1991.

Thompson, Wendy. *Ludwig van Beethoven.* New York: Viking, 1990.

Weil, Lisl. *New Clothes: What People Wore, From Cavemen to Astronauts.* New York: Atheneum, 1987.

ON-LINE INFORMATION*

www.historyabout.com
The History Net has a wide range of history topics and articles around the world that are continually updated.

www.fordham.edu
The Internet Modern History Sourcebook from Fordham University has original document sources on the scientific, political, and Industrial Revolutions of the late 18th and early 19th centuries.

www.history.evansville.net
The Development of Western Civilization series has good articles on the Age of Revolutions and the Age of Industry.

www.americaslibrary.gov
The Library of Congress site has information on the history of America, including the Lewis and Clark Expedition and the Barbary War.

www.spartacus.schoolnet.co.uk
This Encyclopedia of British History, 1700–1850 has many useful articles on topics ranging from the Industrial Revolution to the African slave trade.

www.acn.net.au
Contains a short history of Australia and many links to other sites and articles.

www.nationalgeographic.com/lewisclark
An interactive tour of the Lewis and Clark Expedition.

www.wus.edu
Information on Japan in the 17th to 19th centuries during the Tokugawa shogunate.

www.napoleonbonaparte.nl
The Napoleon Bonaparte Internet Guide offers a comprehensive guide to Napoleonic sites on the Web.

Websites change from time to time. For additional on-line information, check with the media specialist at your local library.

ABOUT THE AUTHOR

Ruth Ashby was educated at Yale University and the University of Virginia, where she studied Victorian literature and culture. Ever since she read *Pride and Prejudice* at age twelve, she has been fascinated by the way people lived two hundred years ago. She has written more than fifteen nonfiction books for young people, including *Elizabethan England* (Benchmark Books 1999), *Victorian England* (Benchmark Books 2003), and *Herstory* (Viking 1995). She hopes to write many more.

INDEX